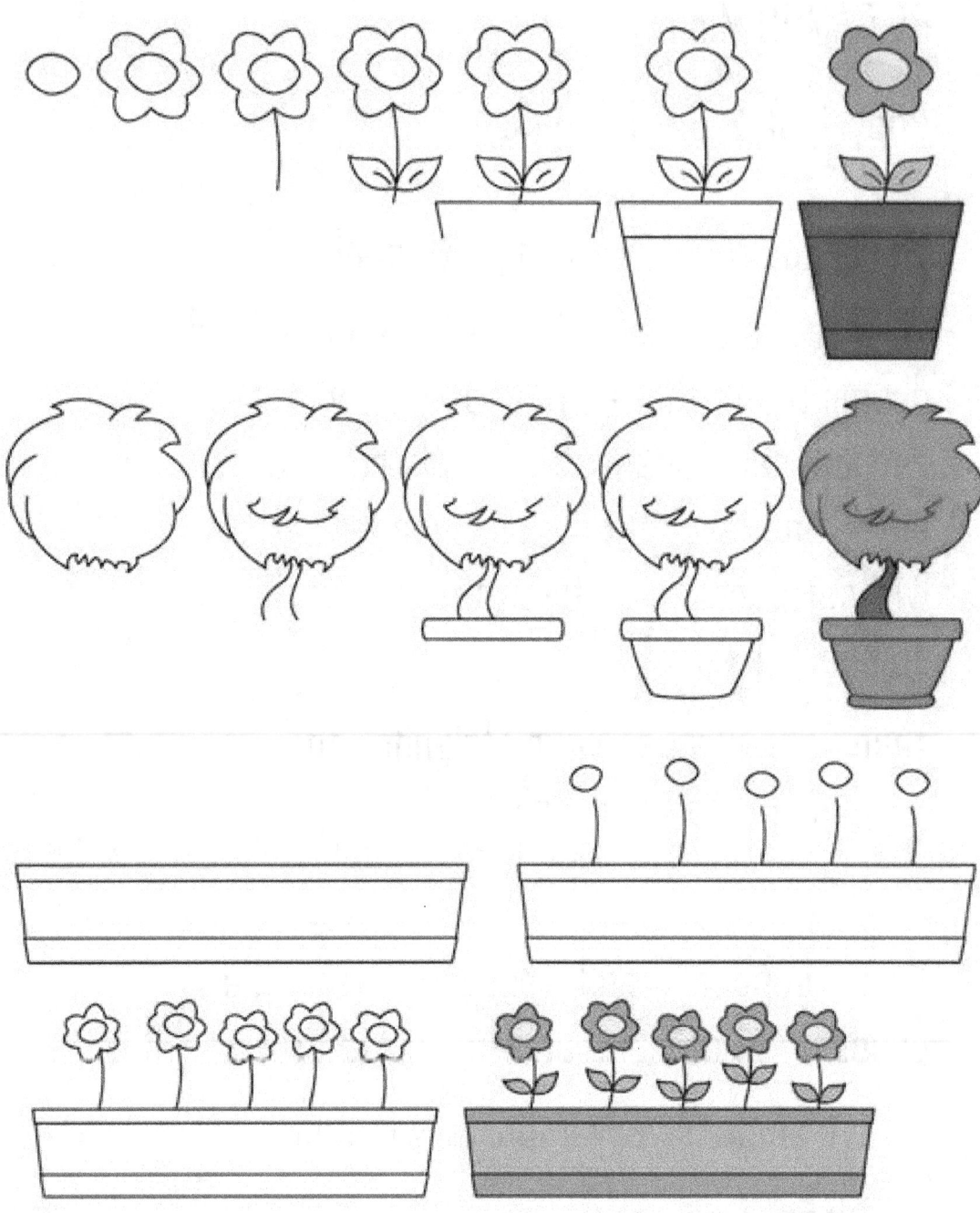

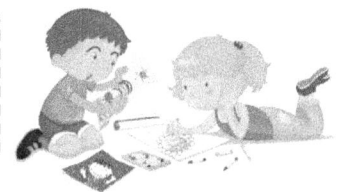

Let's redraw it on our own, my little artists

Let's Draw Our Garden

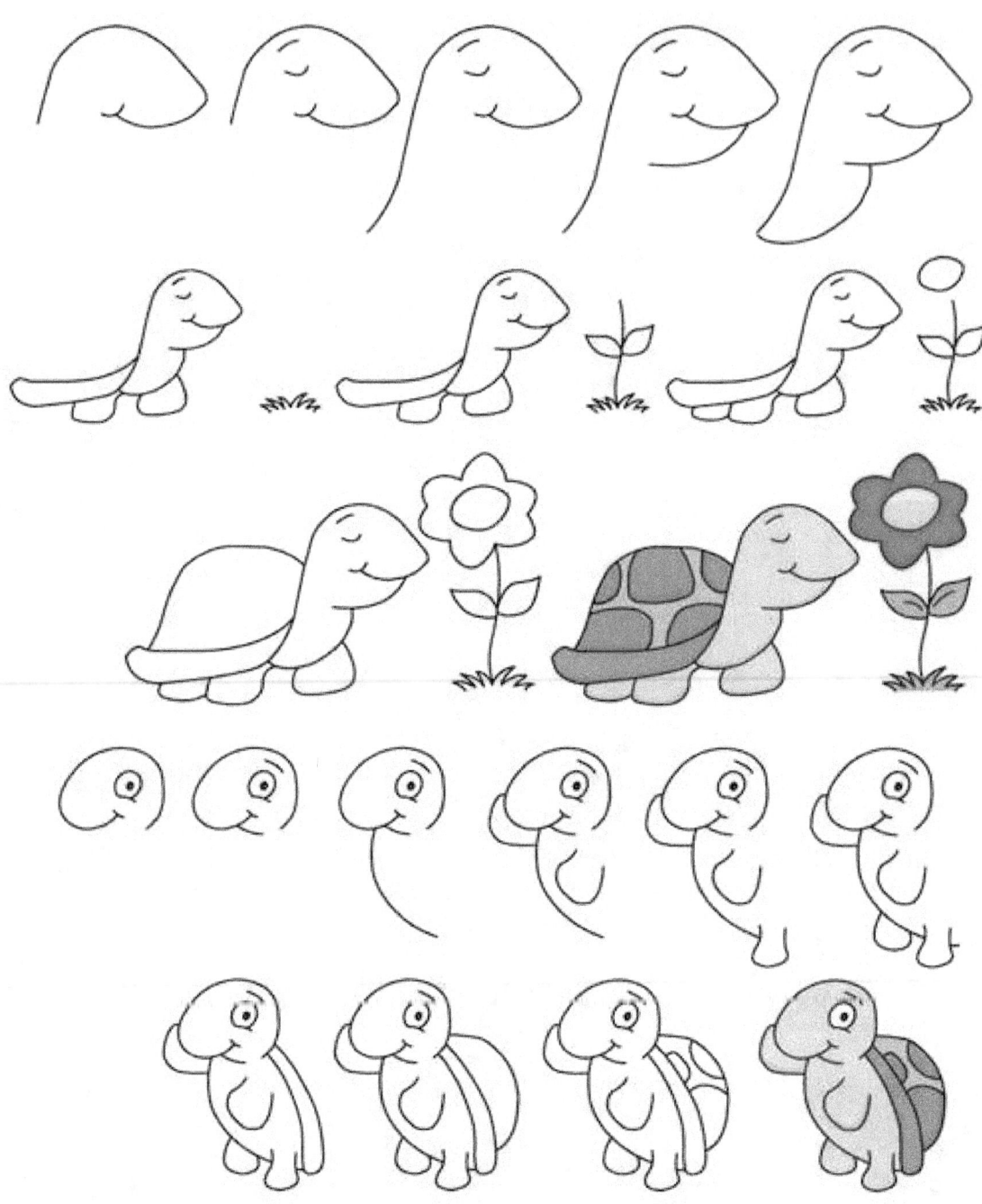

Let's redraw it on our own, my little artists

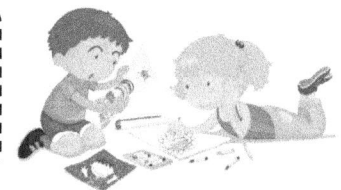

Let's Draw Our Garden

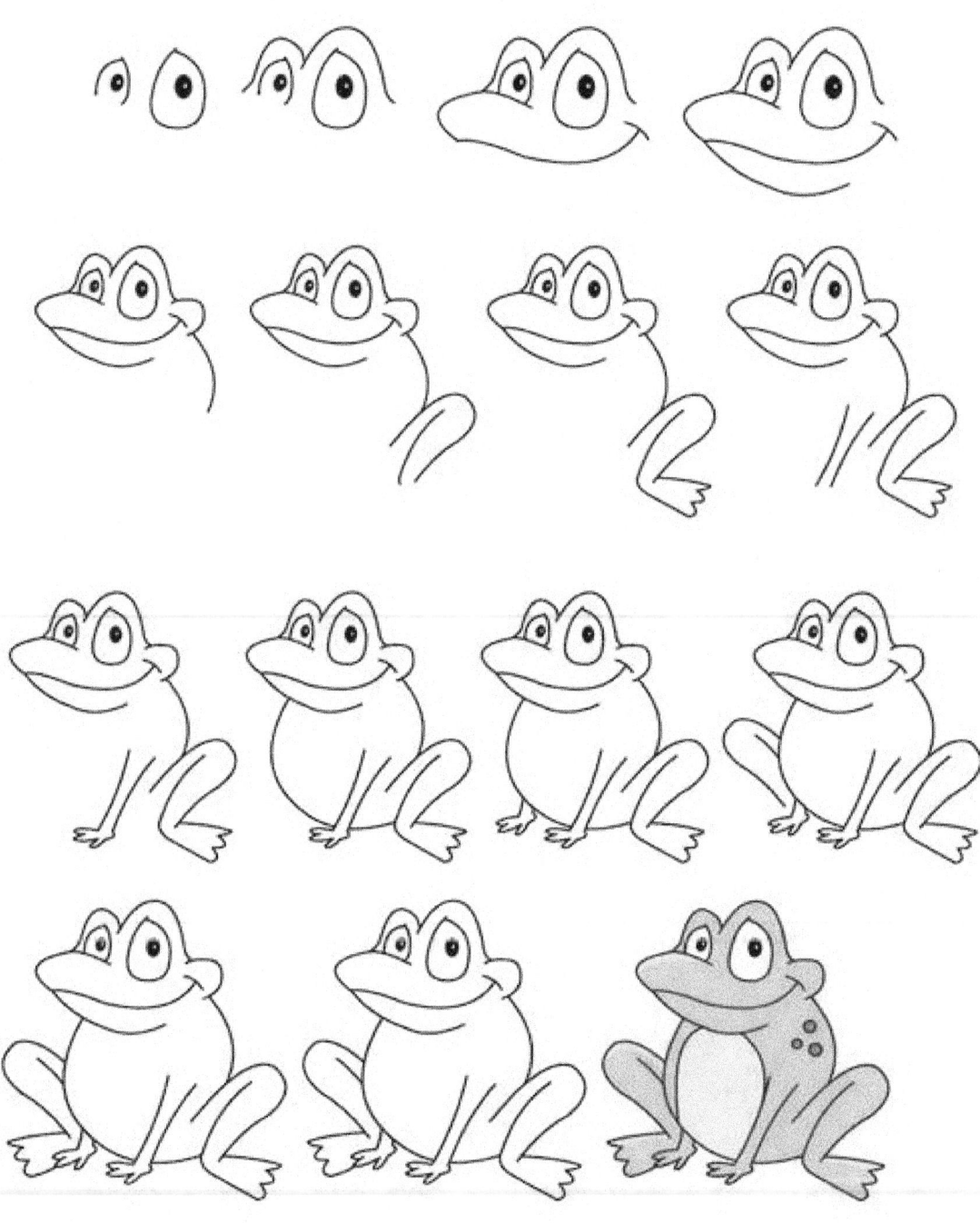

Let's redraw it on our own, my little artists

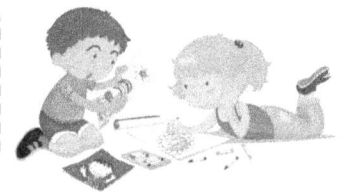

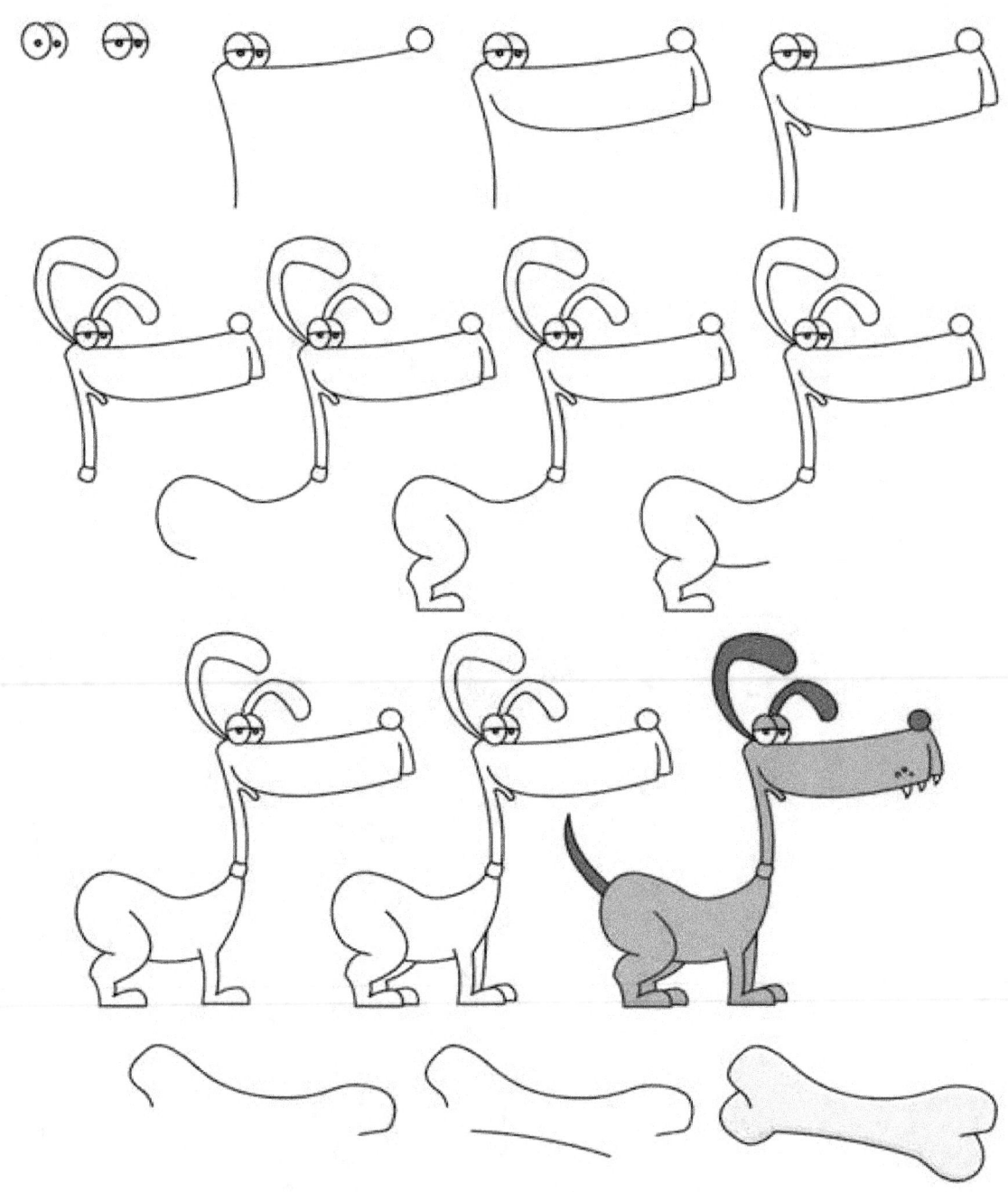

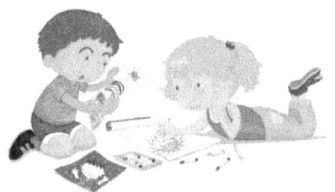

Let's redraw it on our own, my little artists

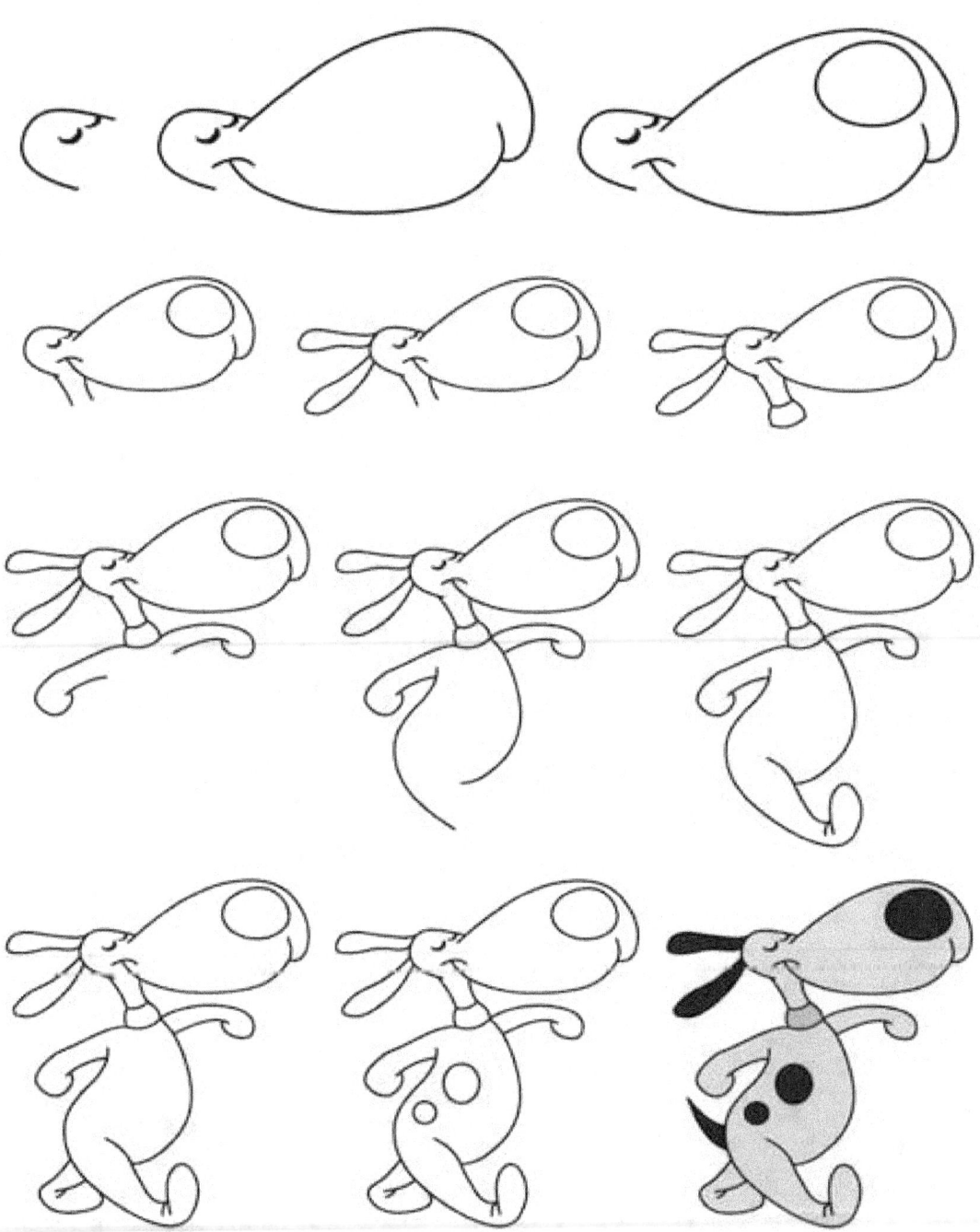

Let's redraw it on our own, my little artists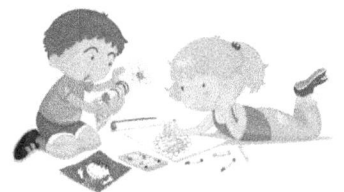

Let's Draw Our Garden

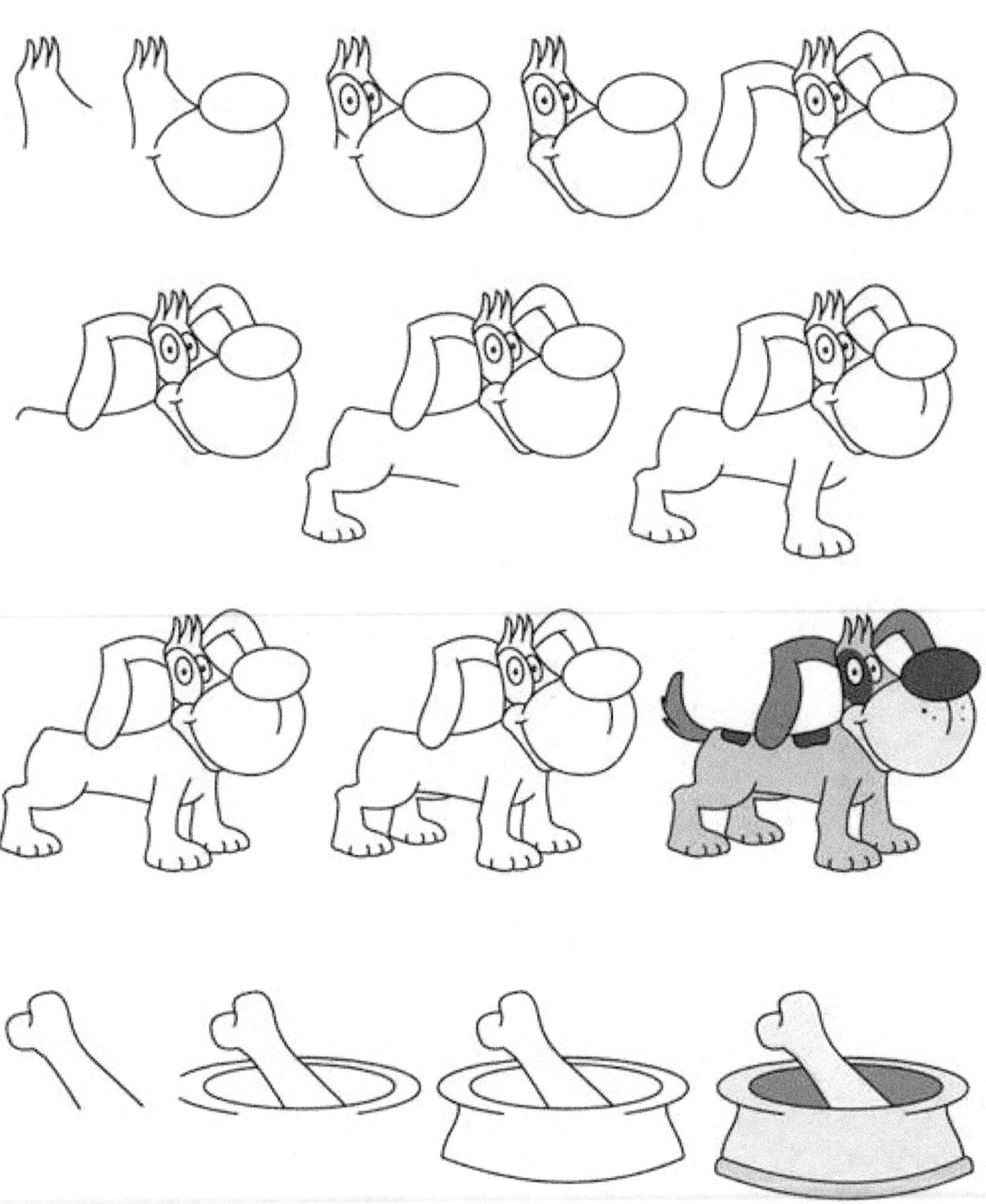

Let's redraw it on our own, my little artists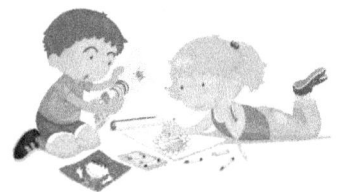

Let's Draw Our Garden

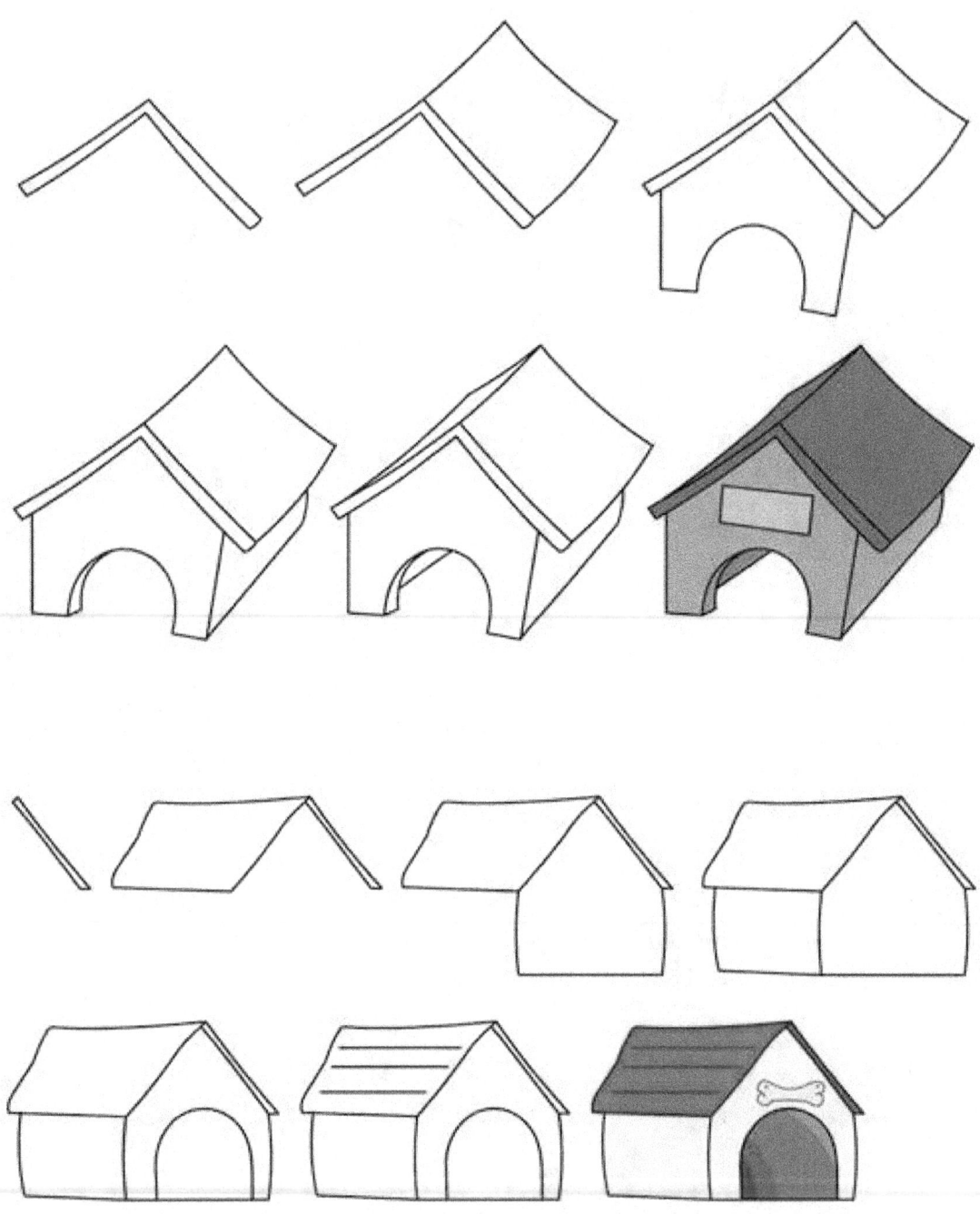

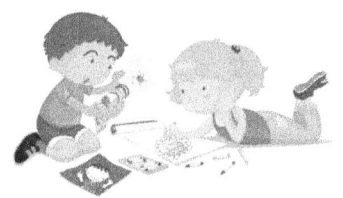

Let's redraw it on our own, my little artists

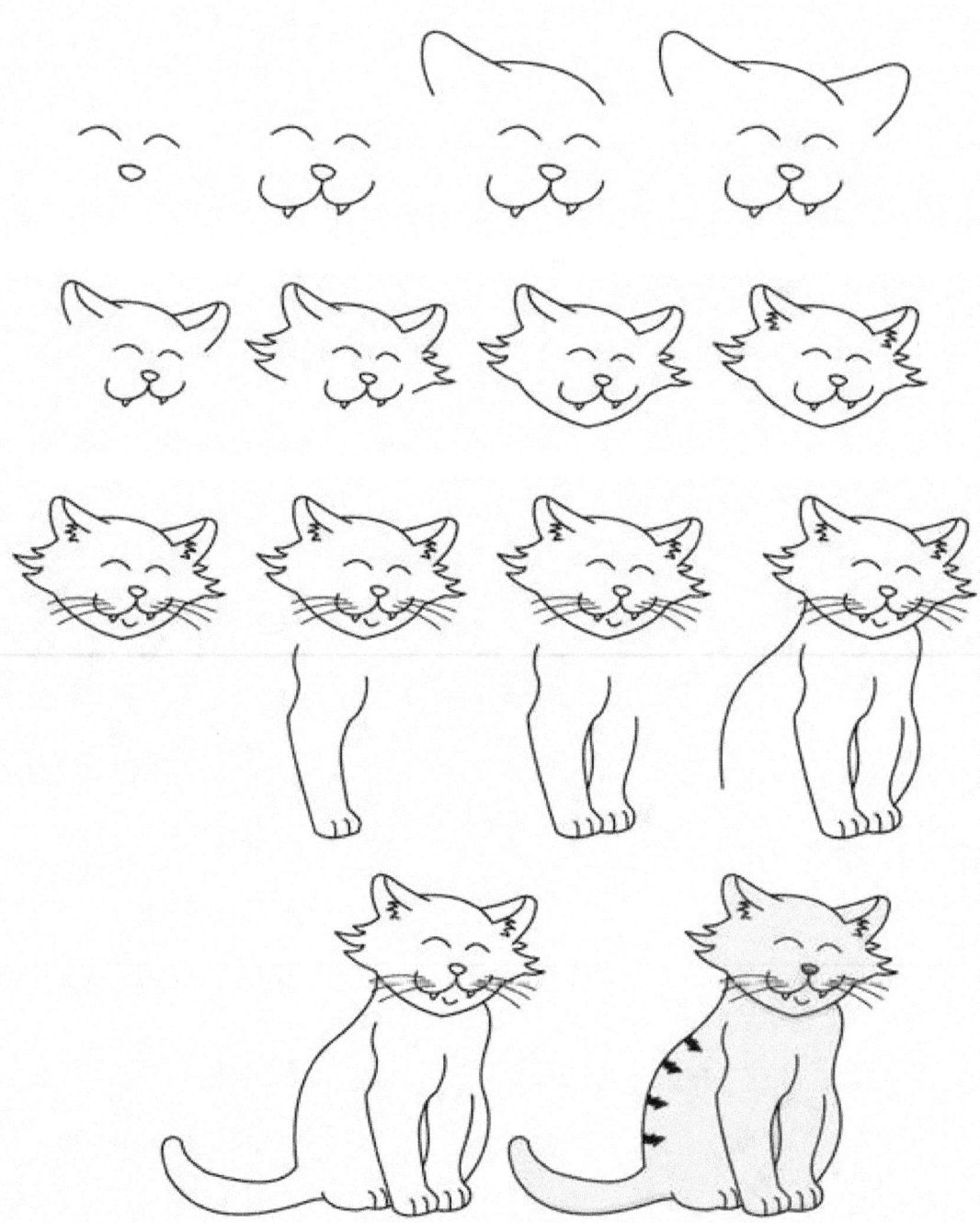

Let's redraw it on our own, my little artists

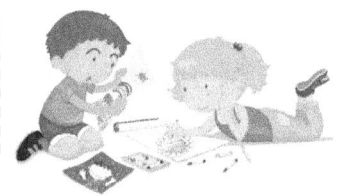

Let's Draw Our Garden

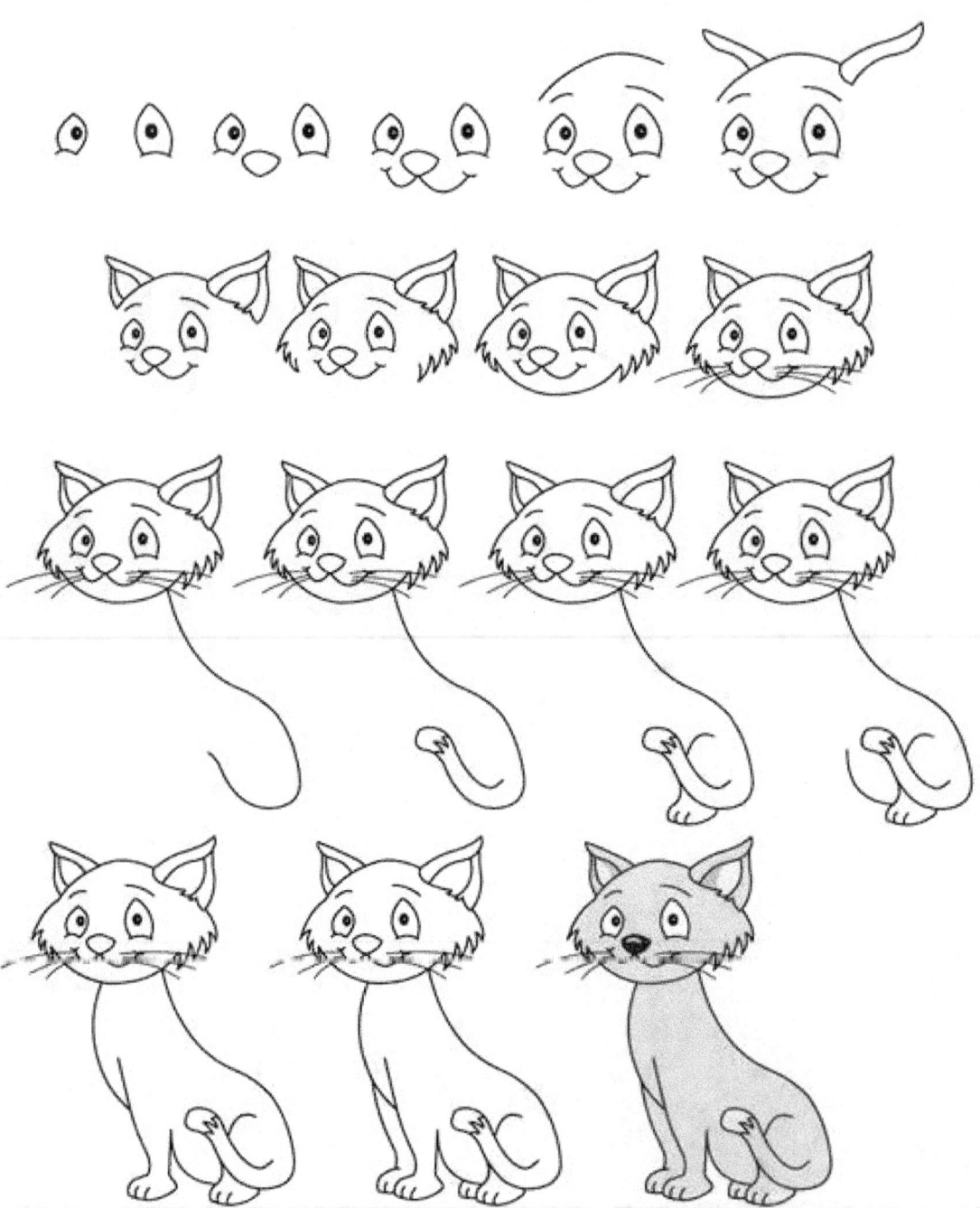

Let's redraw it on our own, my little artists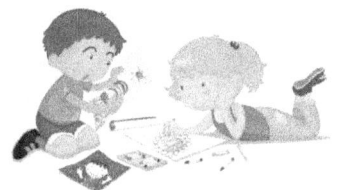

Let's Draw Our Garden

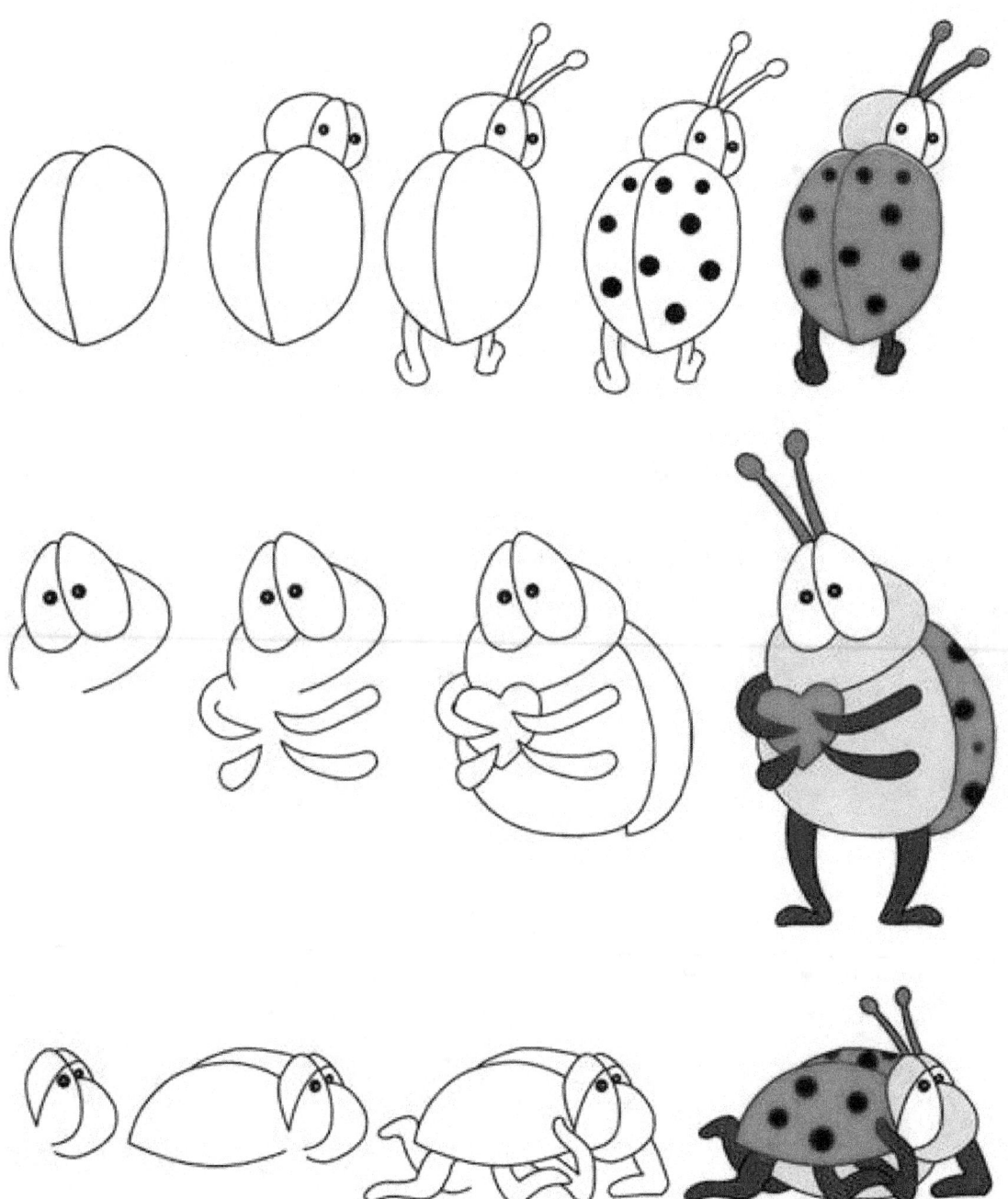

Let's redraw it on our own, my little artists

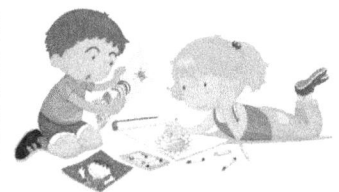

Let's Draw Our Garden

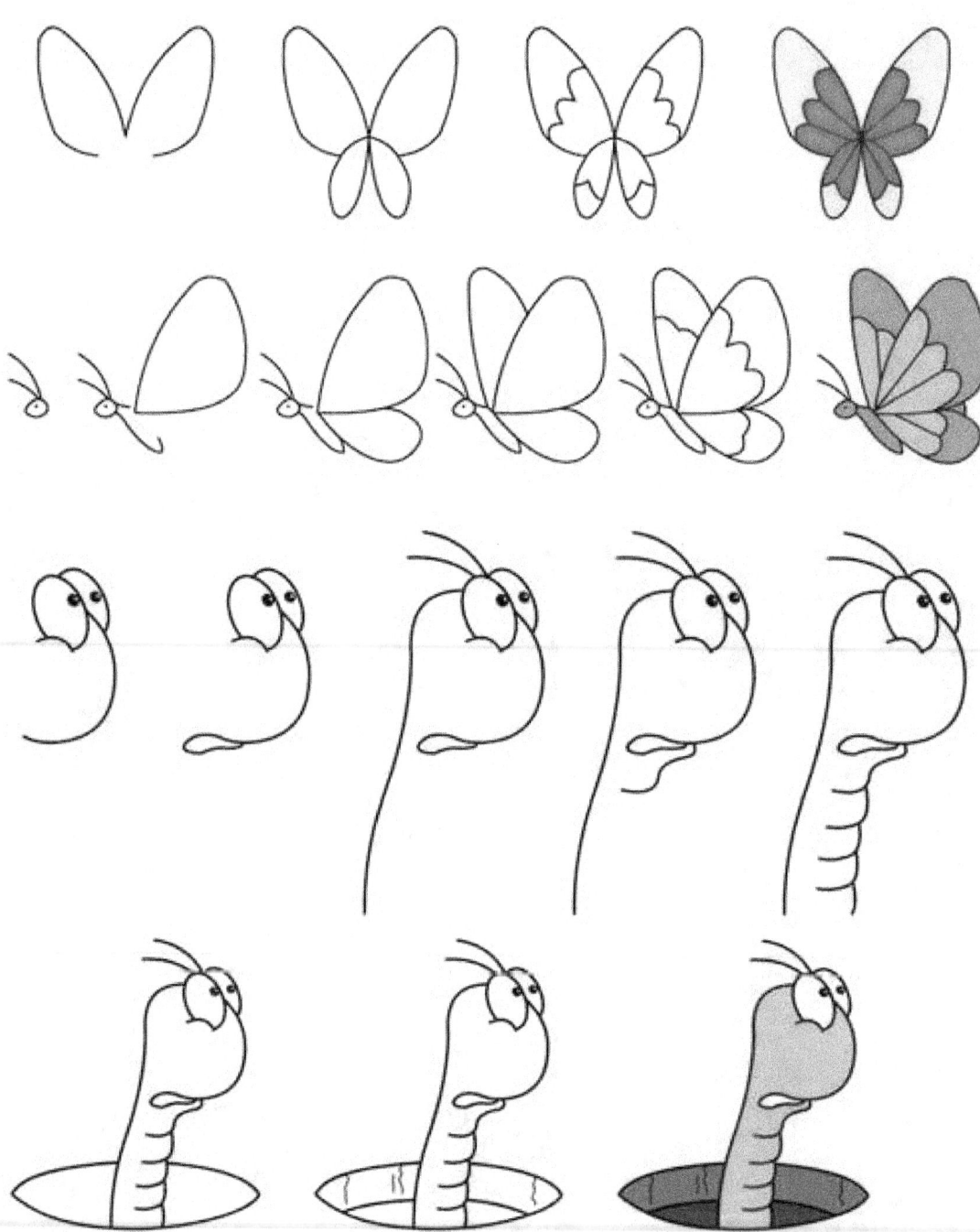

Let's redraw it on our own, my little artists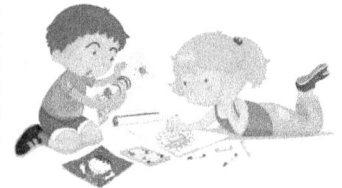

Let's Draw Our Garden

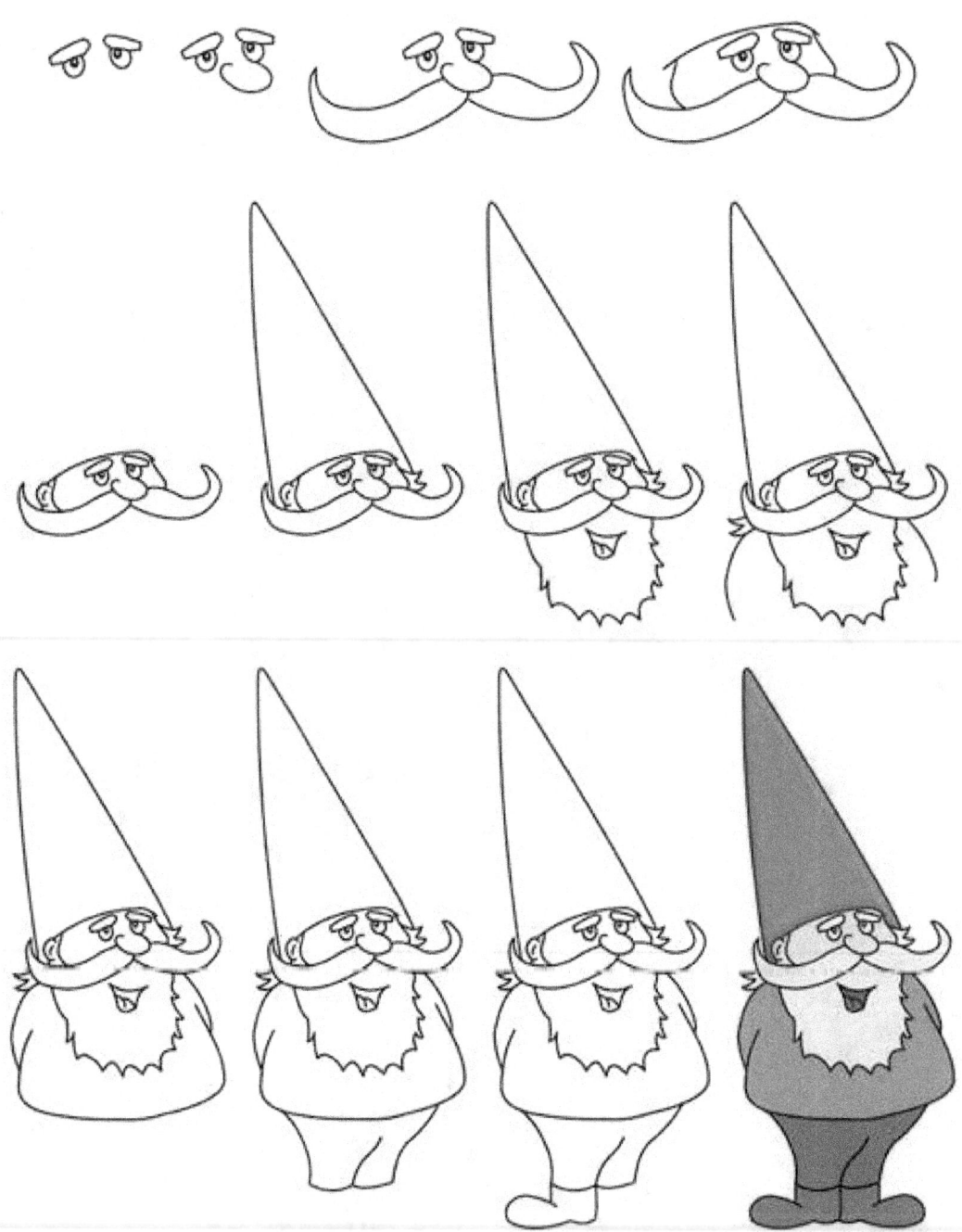

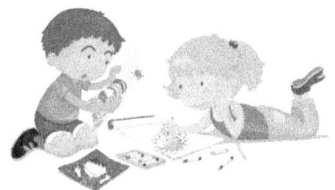

Let's redraw it on our own, my little artists

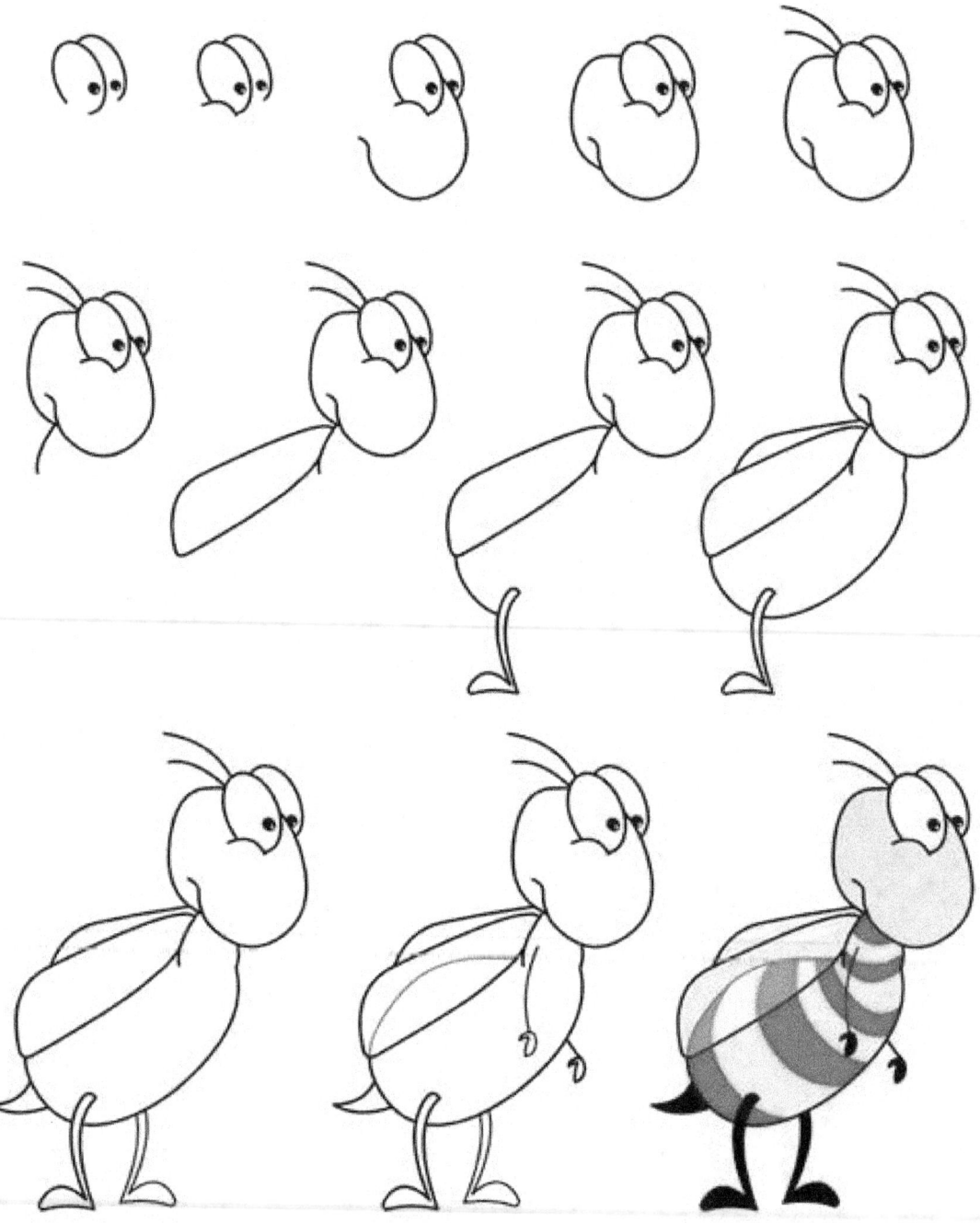

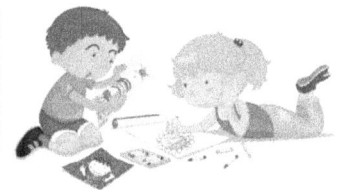

Let's redraw it on our own, my little artists

Let's Draw Our Garden

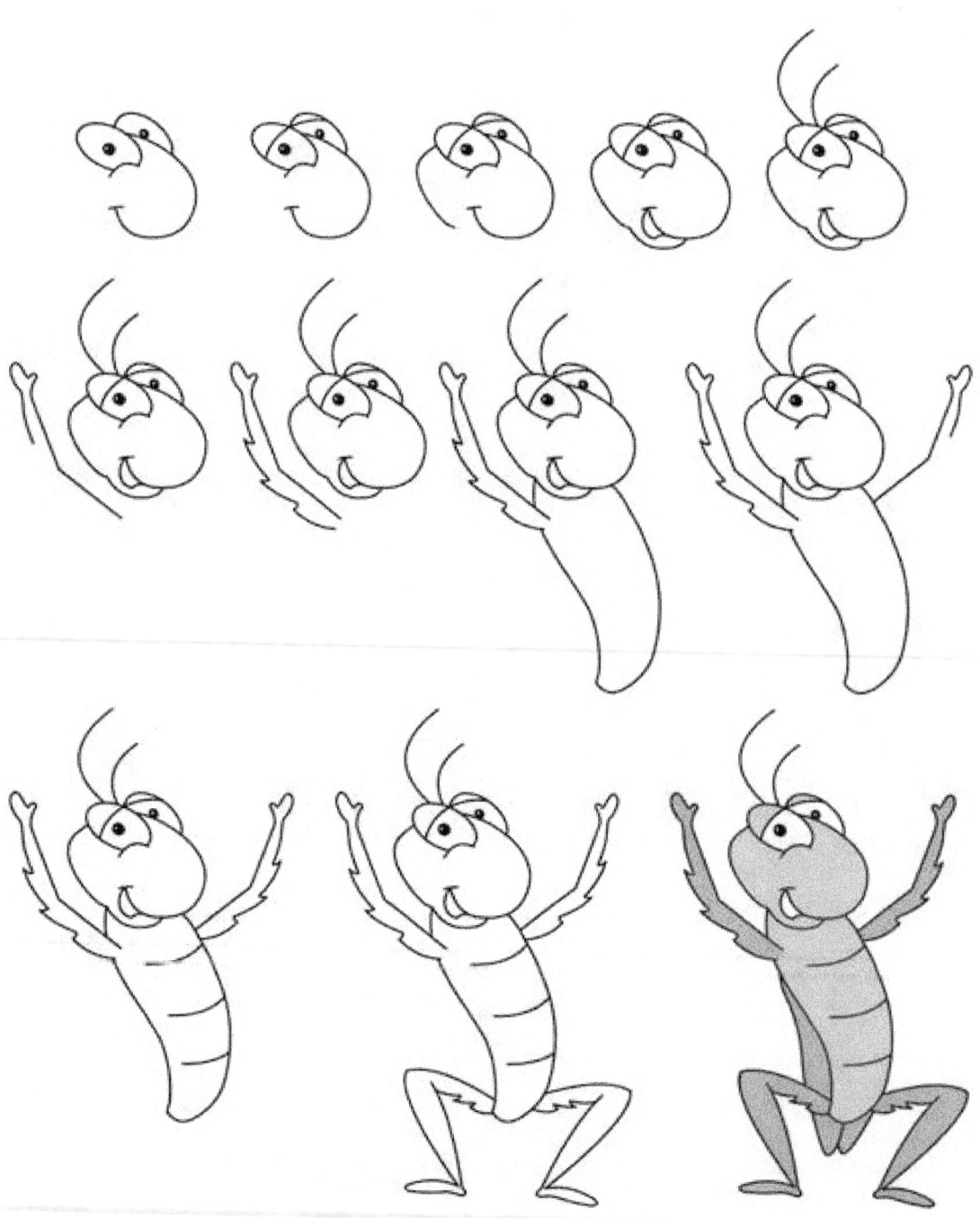

Let's redraw it on our own, my little artists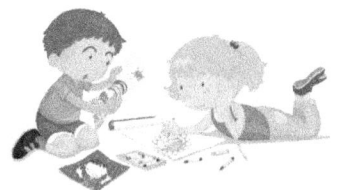

Let's Draw Our Garden

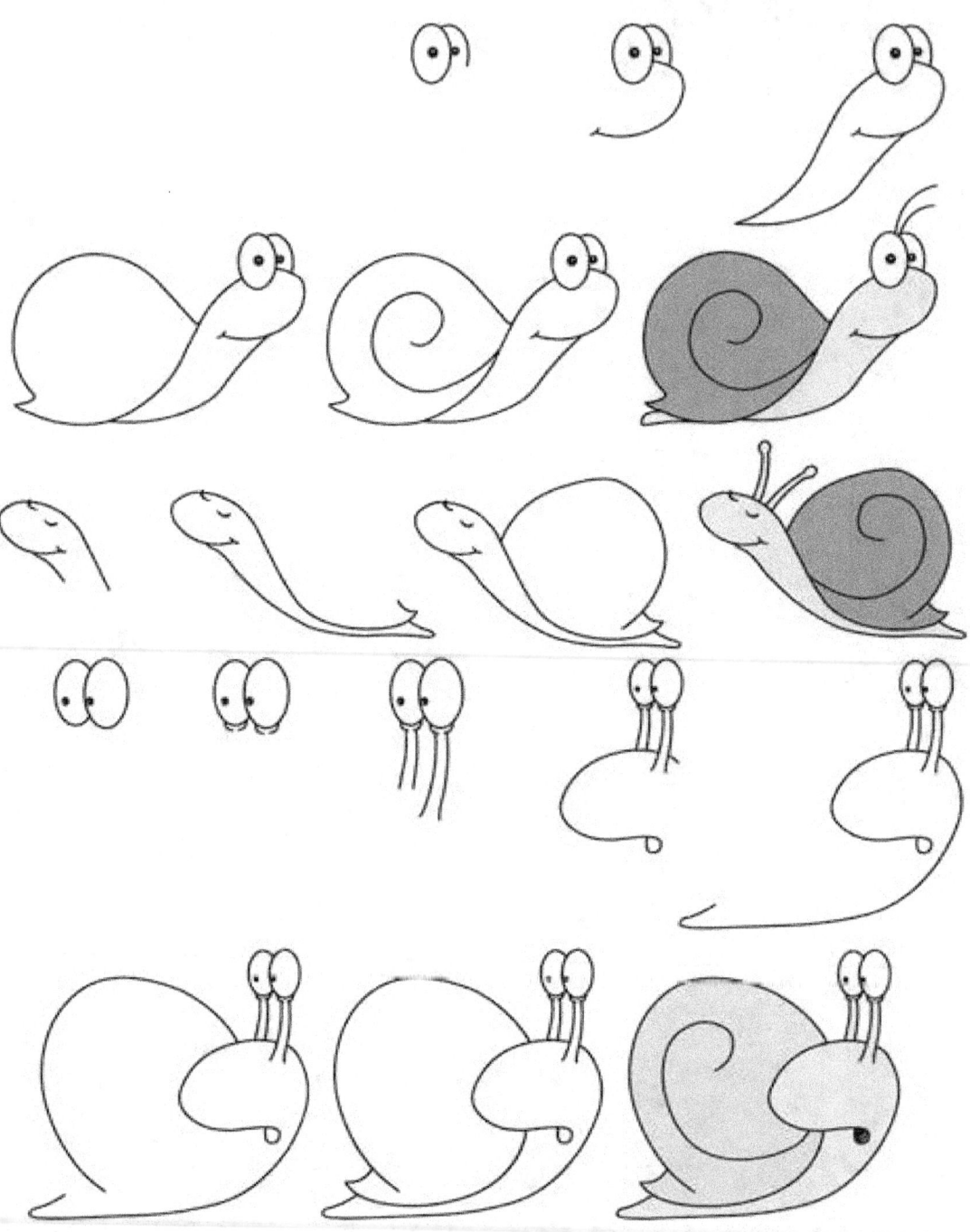

Let's redraw it on our own, my little artists

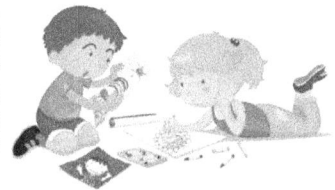

Let's Draw Our Garden

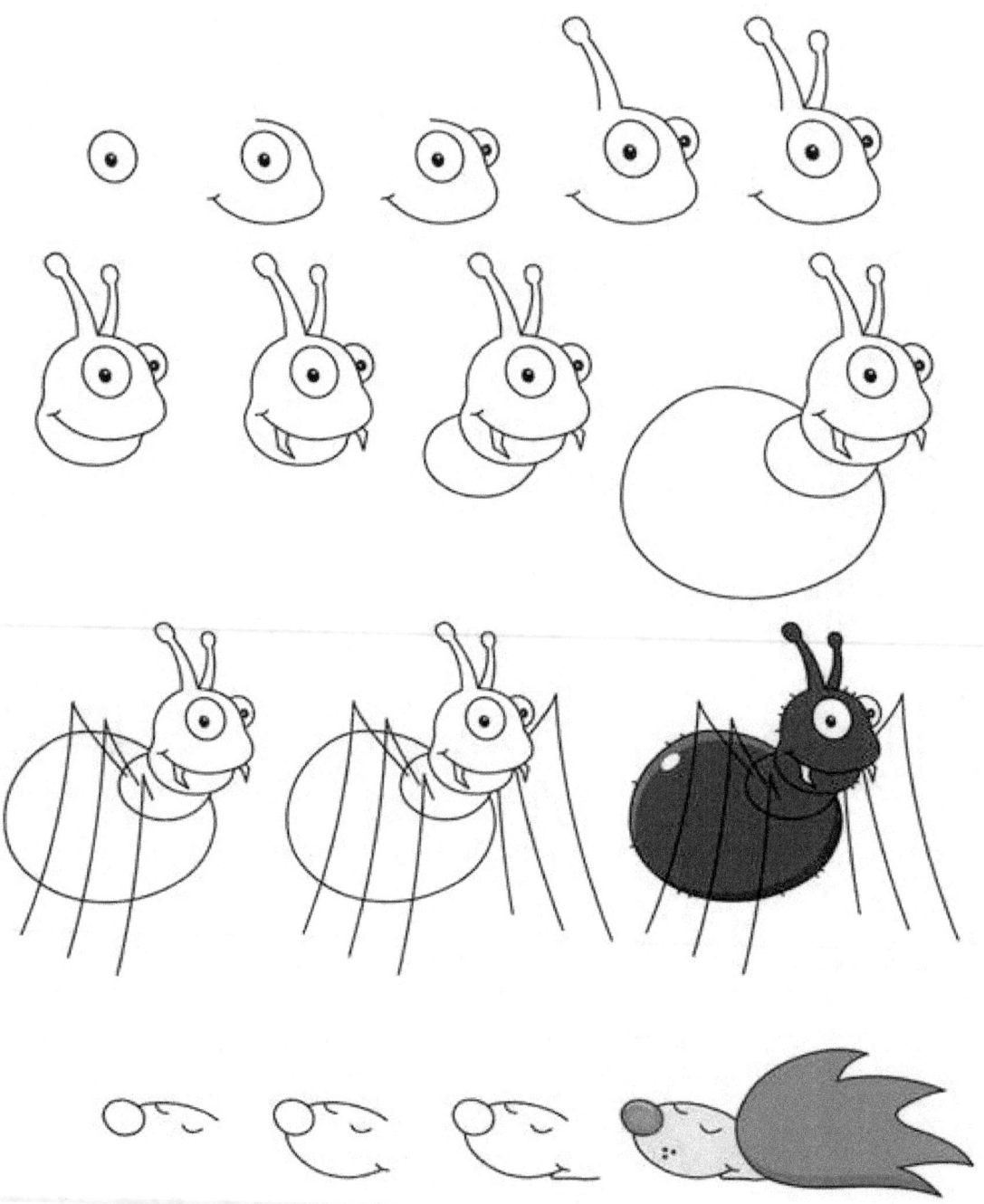

Let's redraw it on our own, my little artists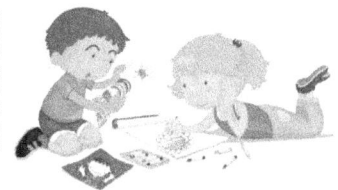

Let's Draw Our Garden

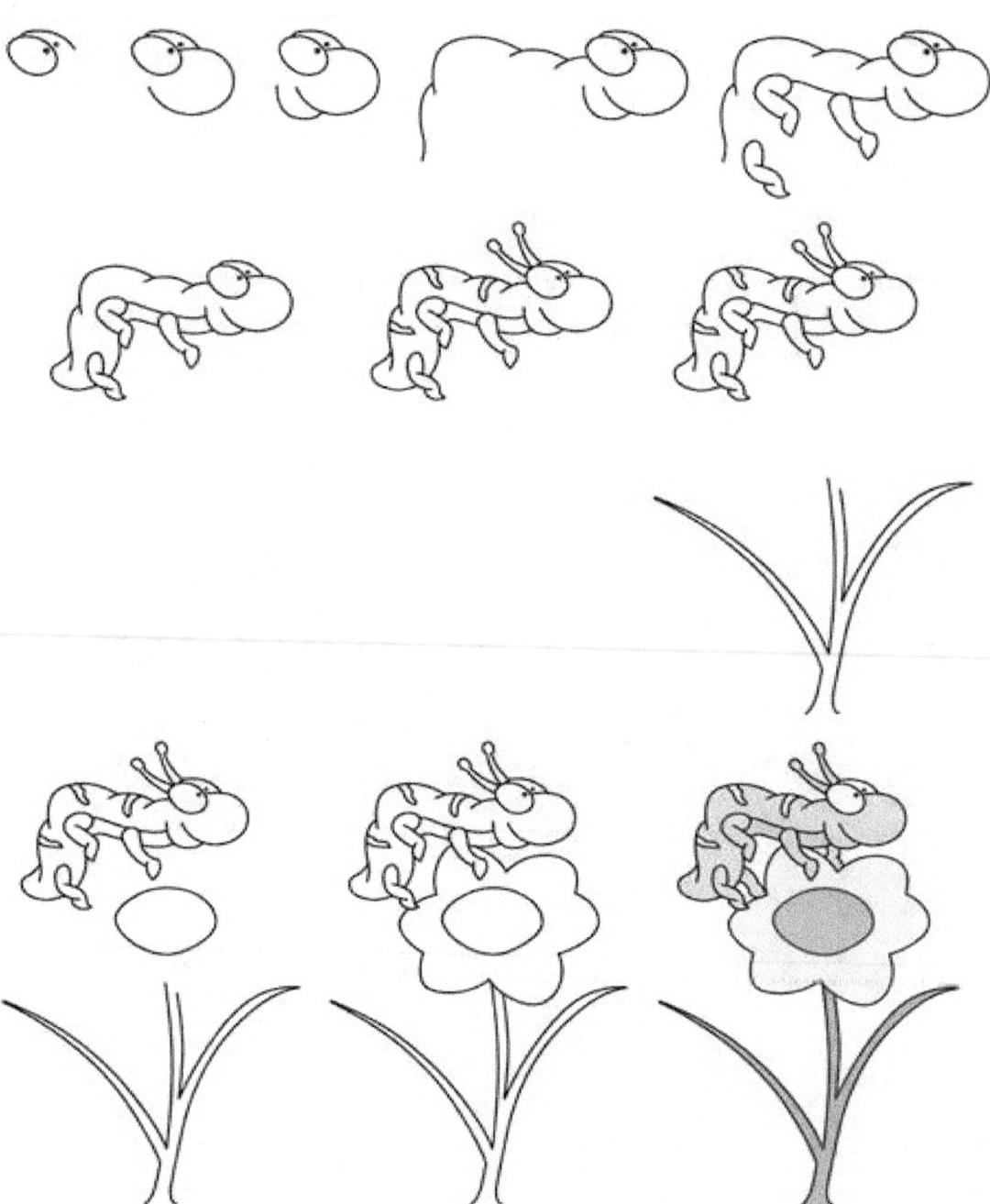

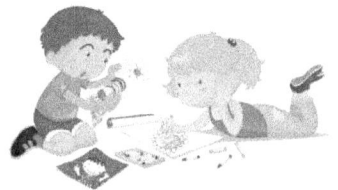

Let's redraw it on our own, my little artists

Let's Draw Our Garden

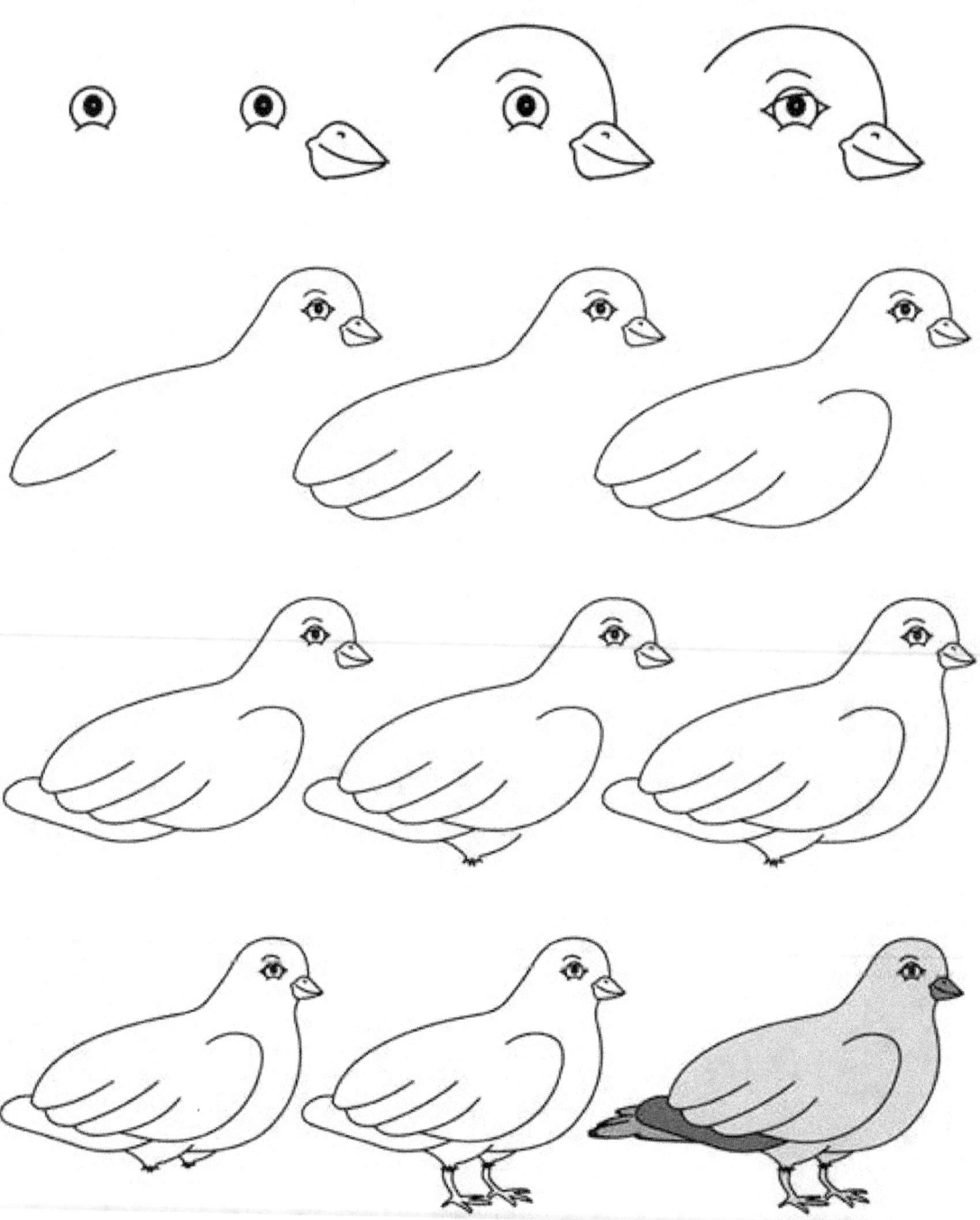

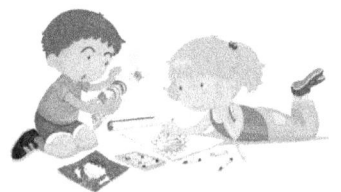

Let's redraw it on our own, my little artists

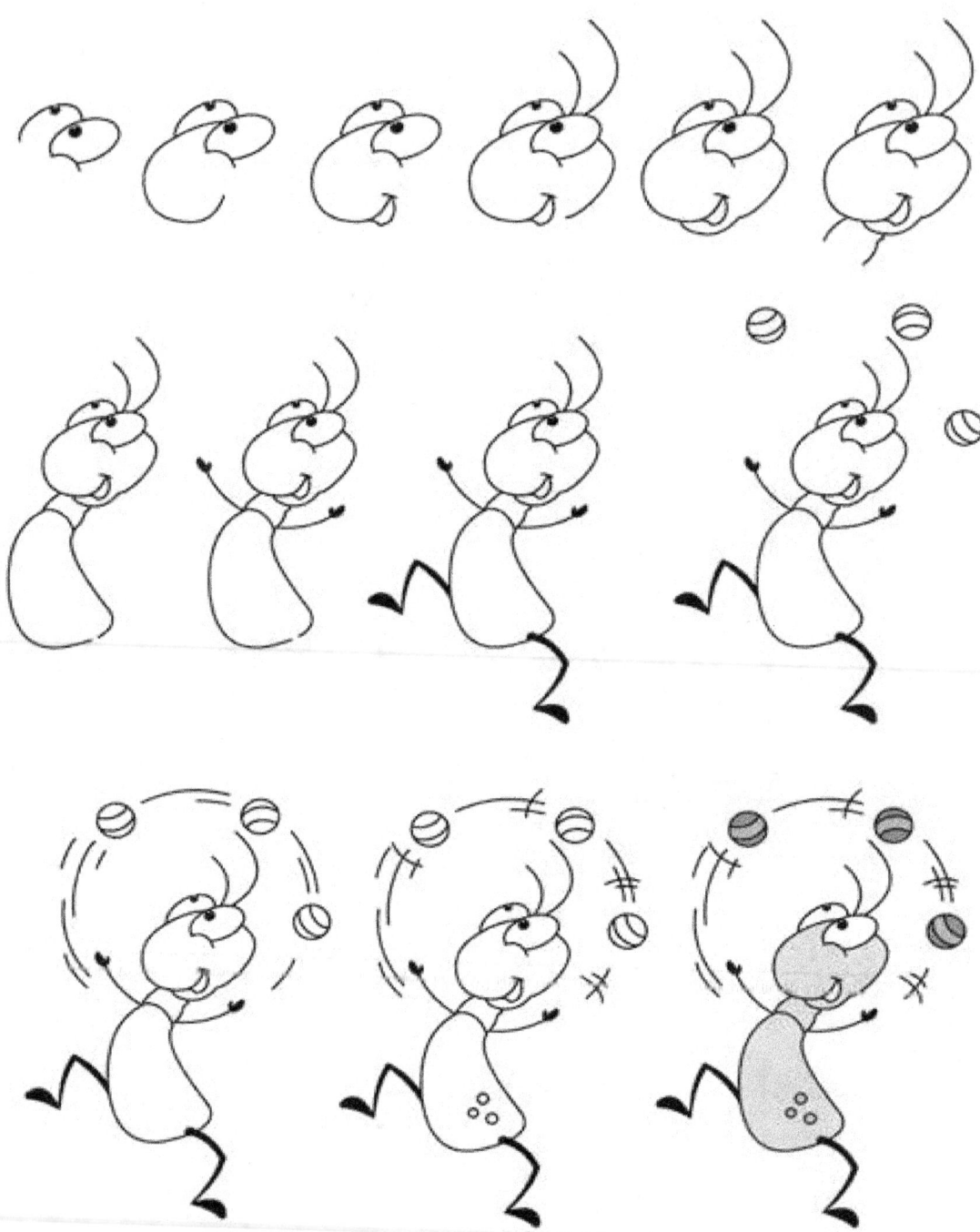

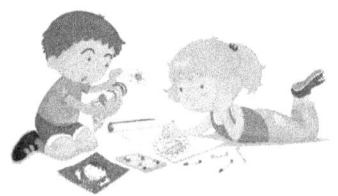

Let's redraw it on our own, my little artists

Let's Draw Our Garden

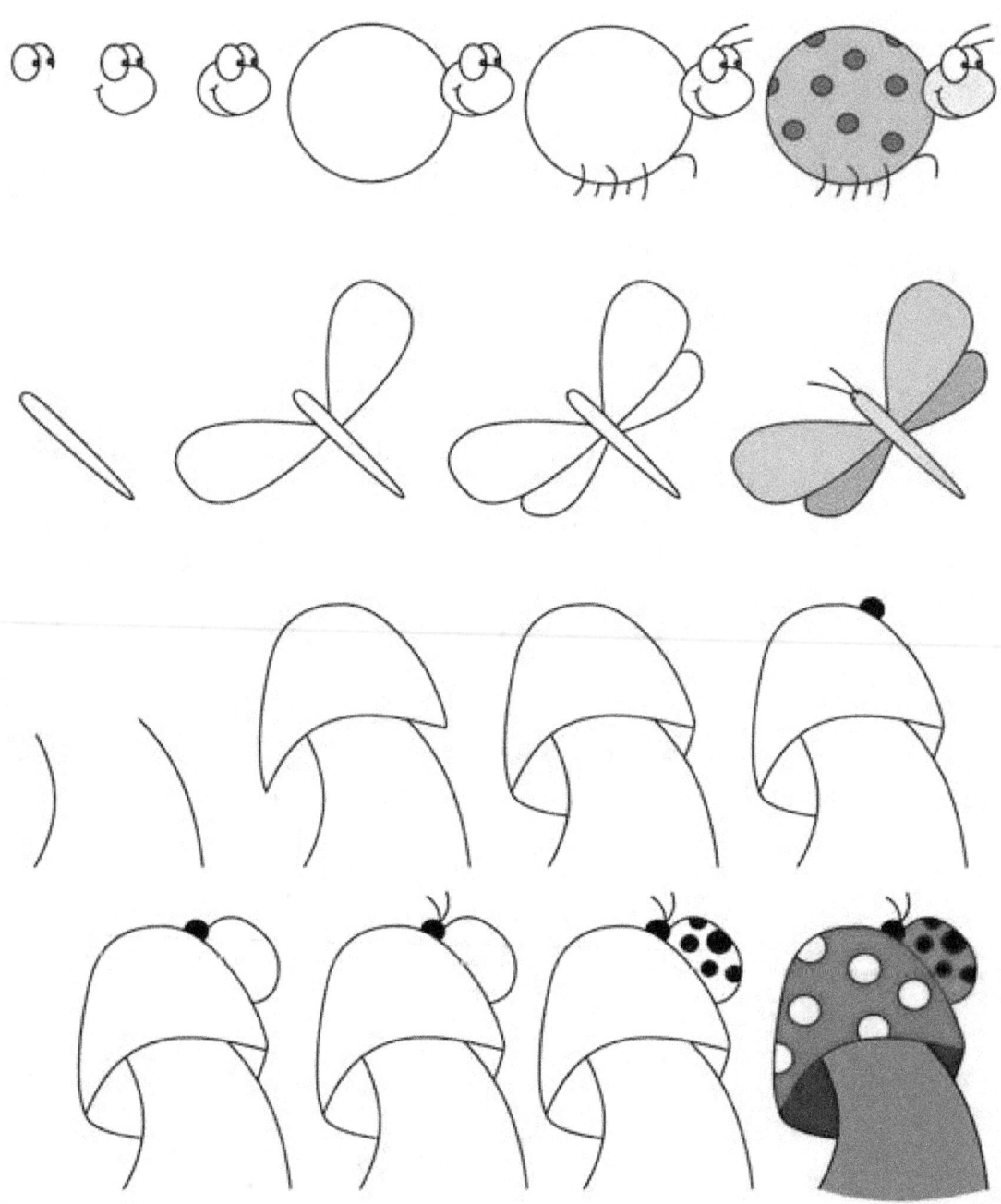

Let's redraw it on our own, my little artists

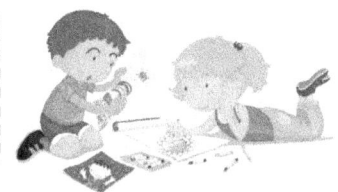

Let's Draw Our Garden

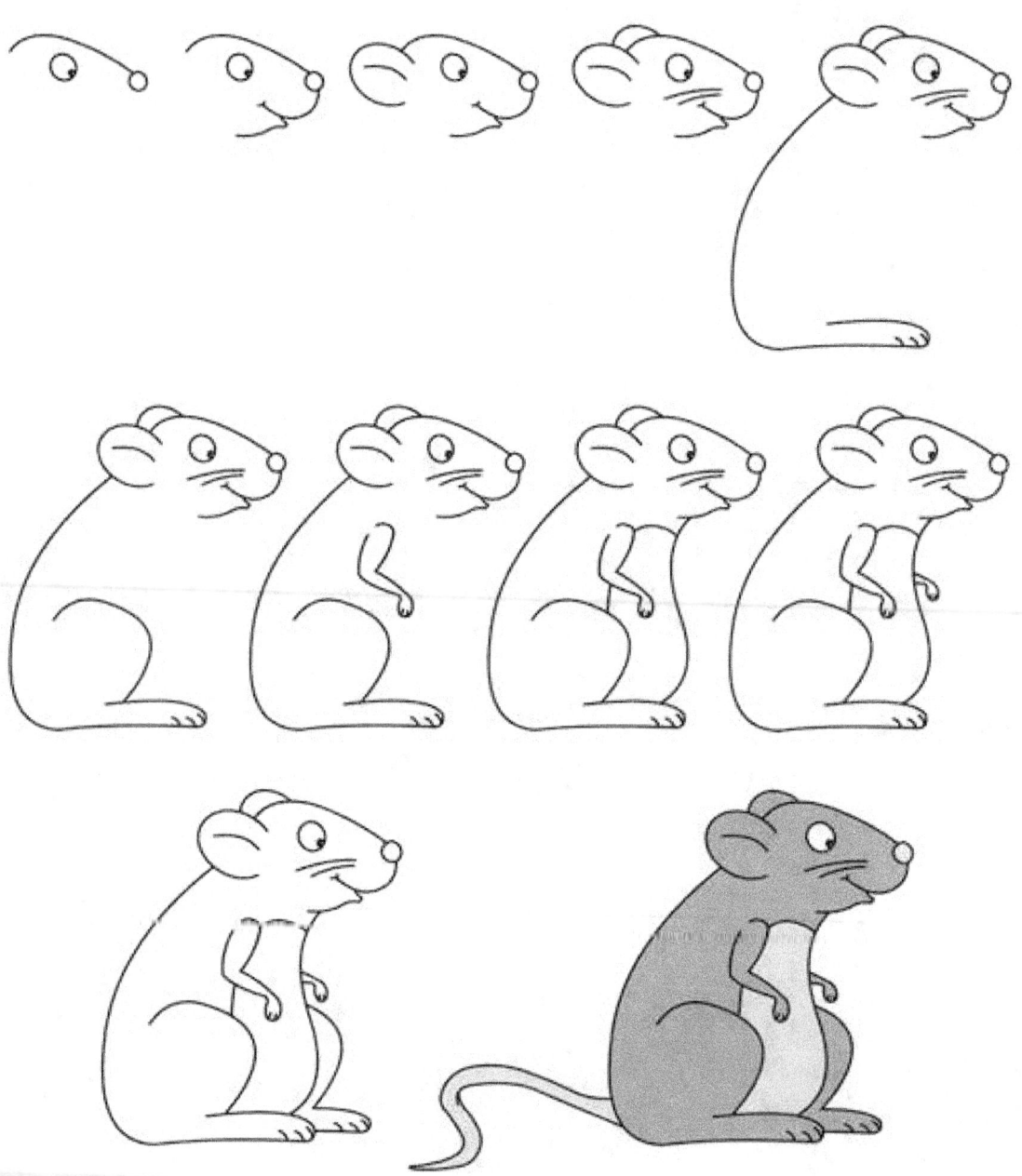

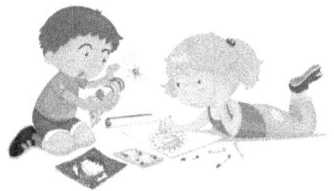

Let's redraw it on our own, my little artists

Let's Draw Our Garden

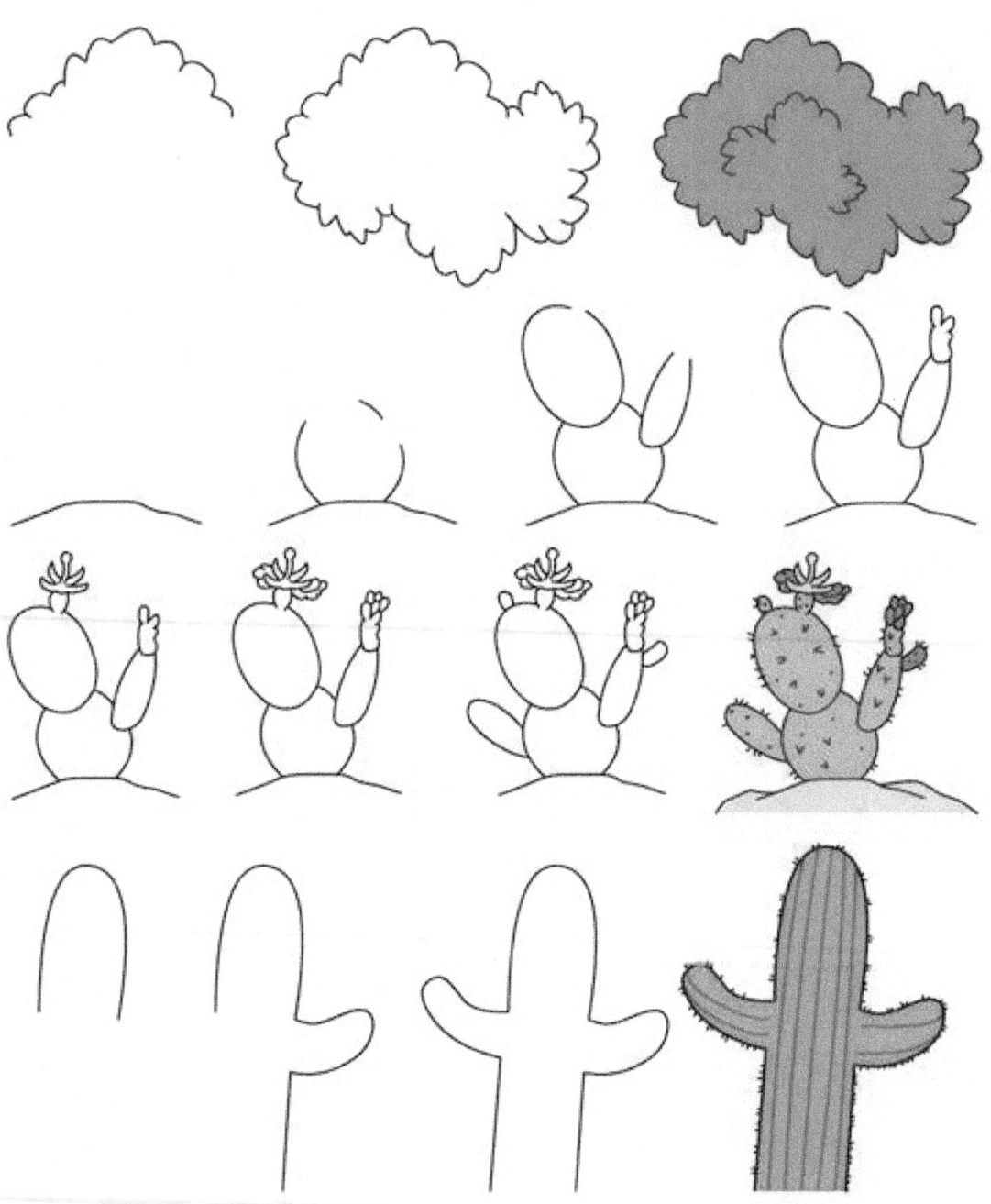

Let's redraw it on our own, my little artists

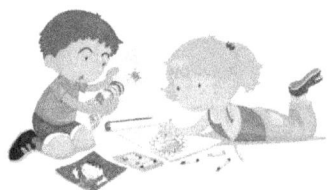

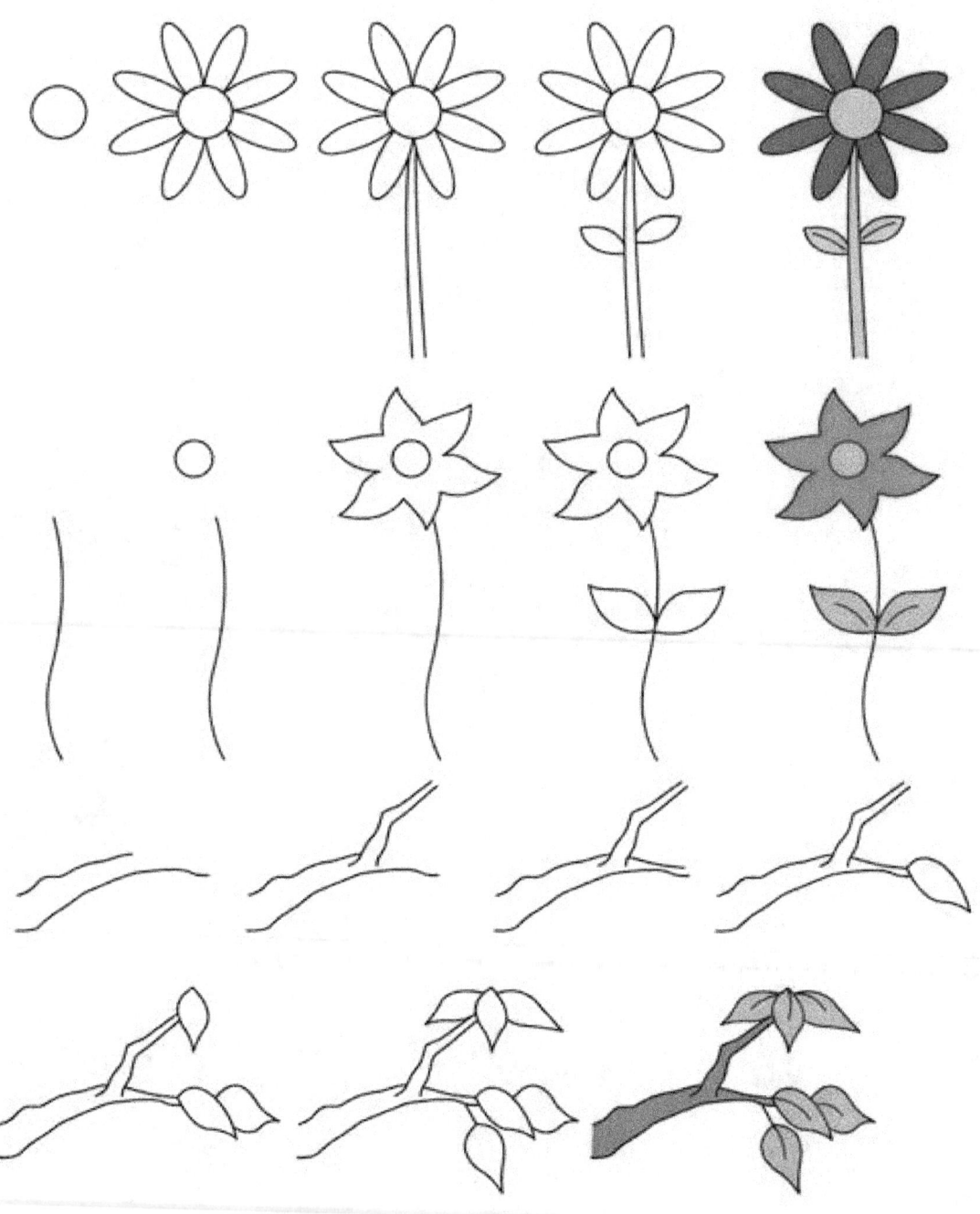

Let's redraw it on our own, my little artists

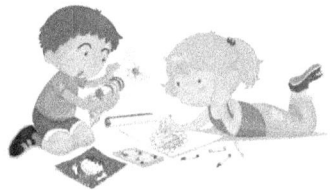

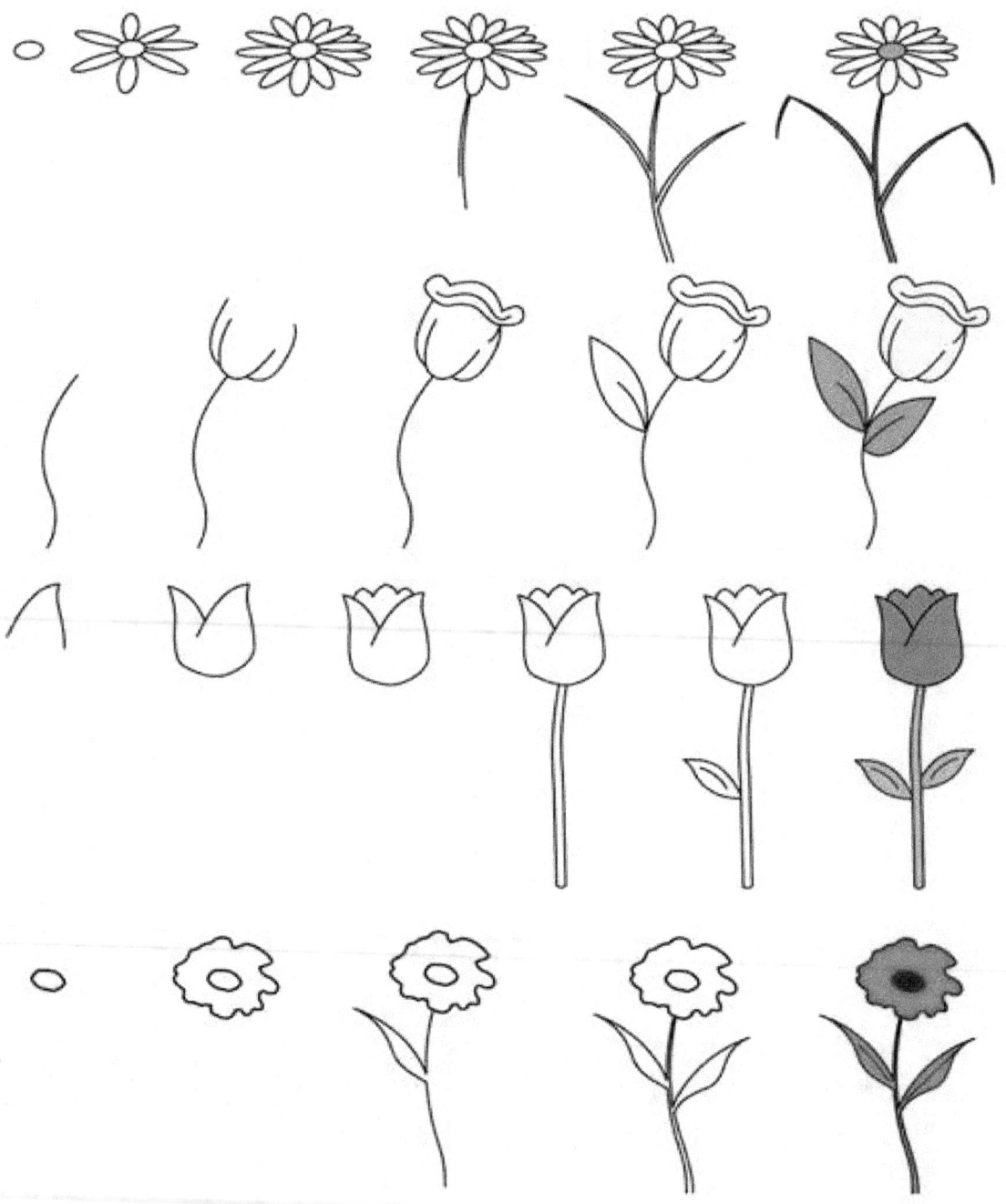

Let's redraw it on our own, my little artists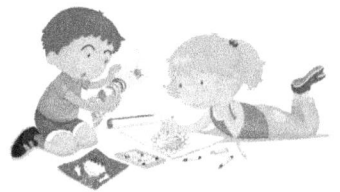

Let's Draw Our Garden

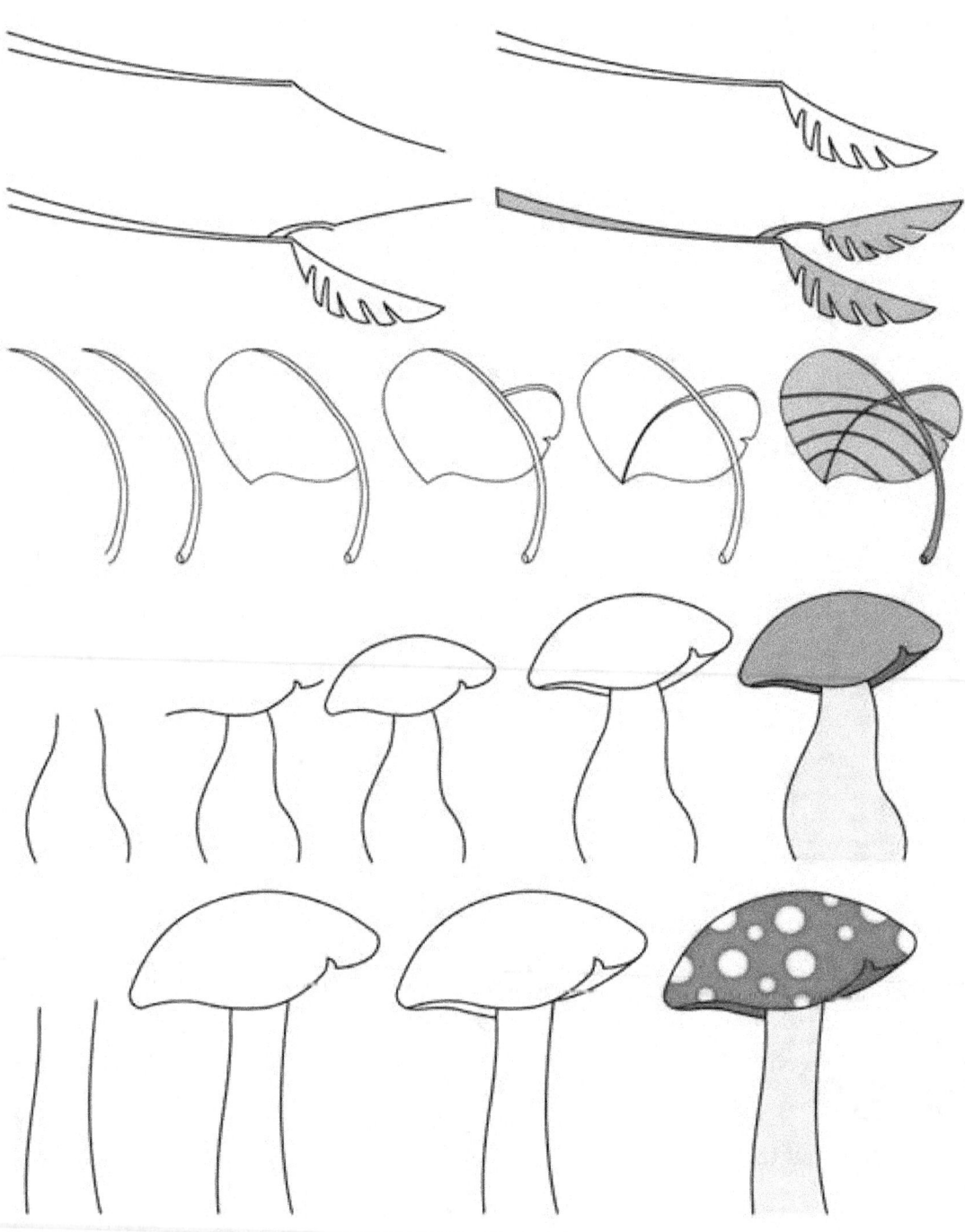

Let's redraw it on our own, my little artists

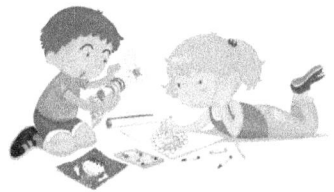

Let's Draw Our Garden

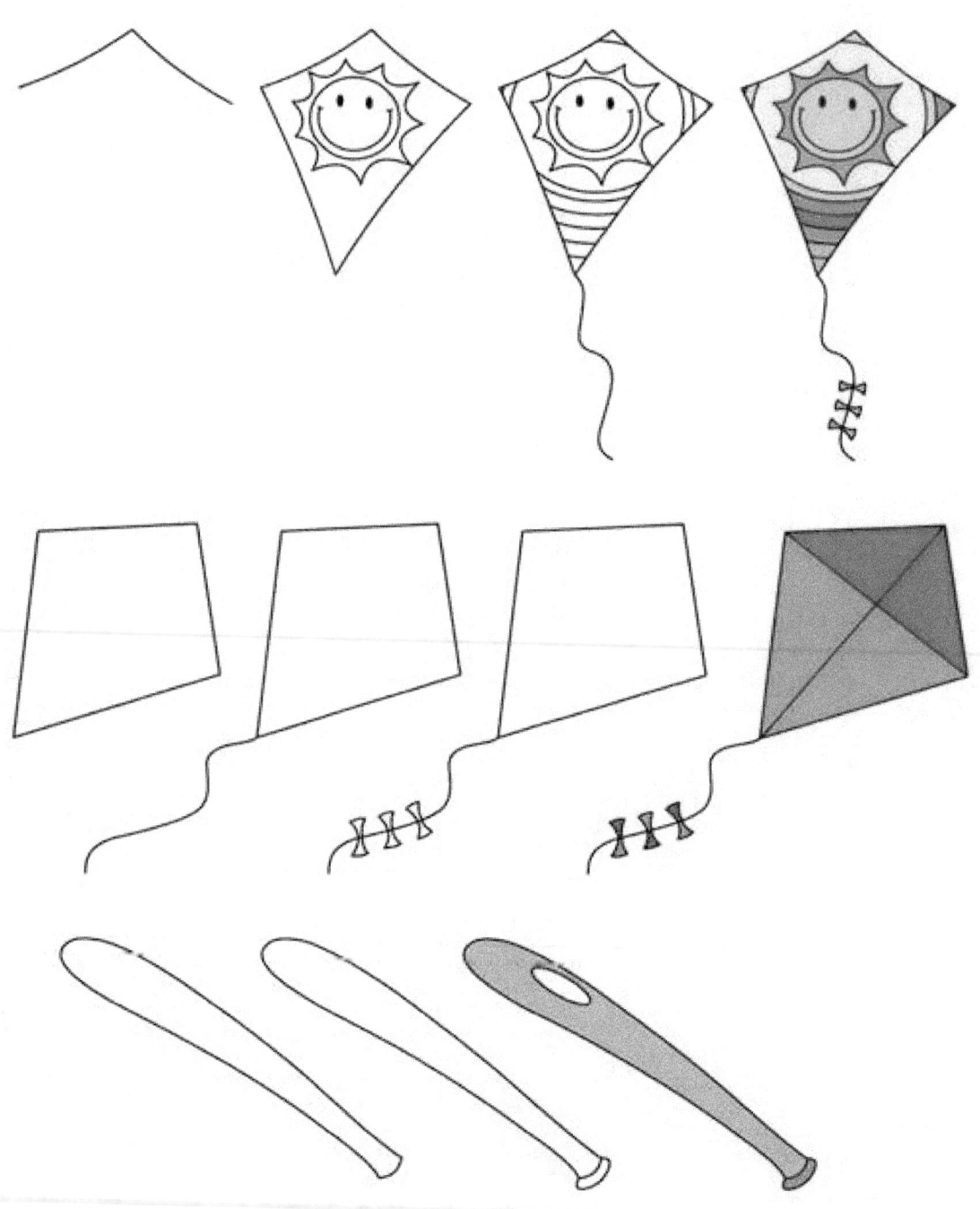

Let's redraw it on our own, my little artists

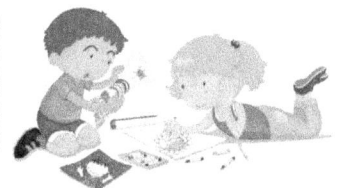

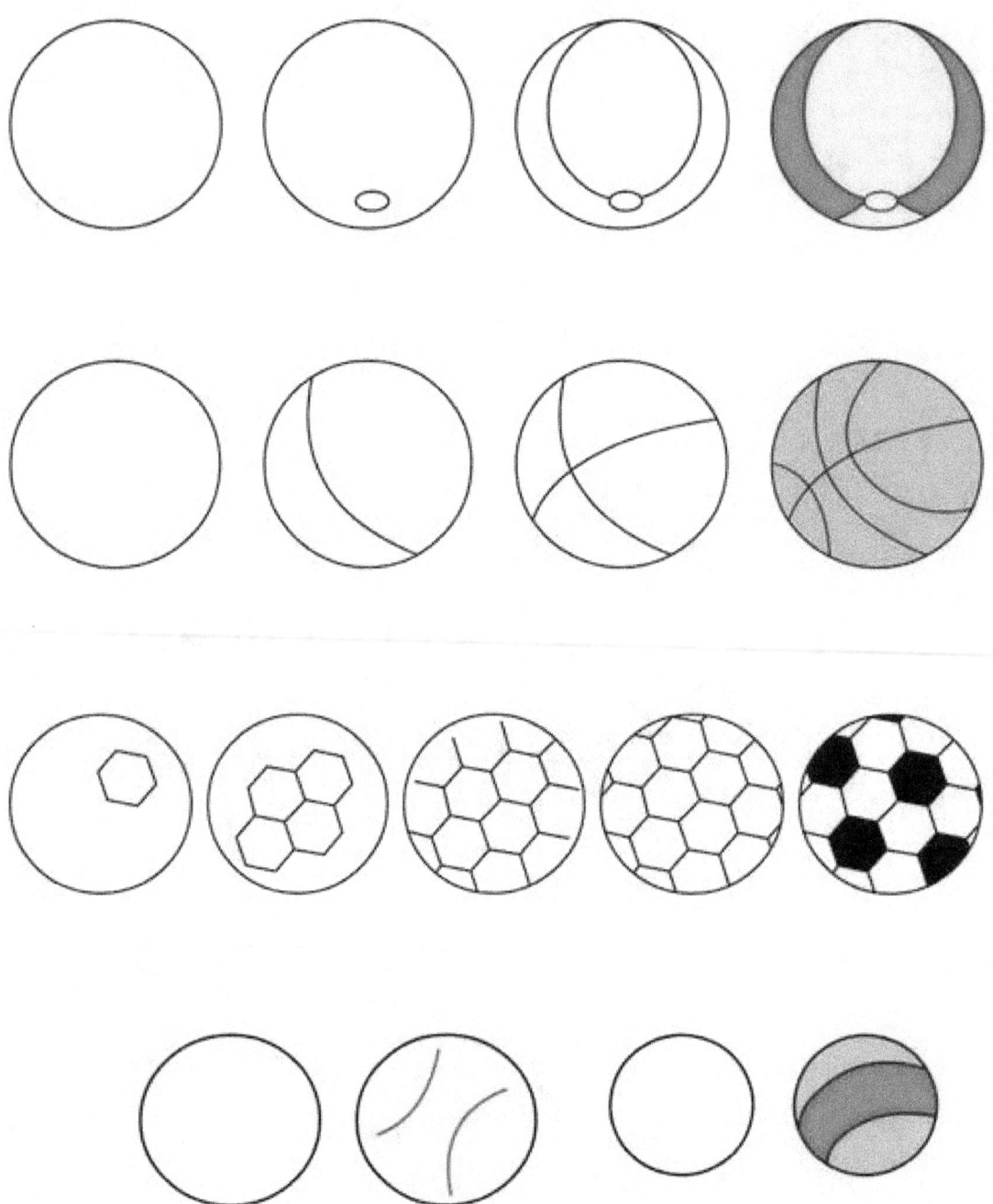

Let's redraw it on our own, my little artists

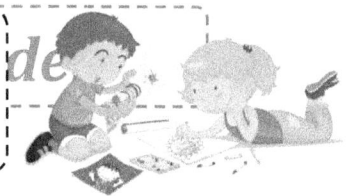

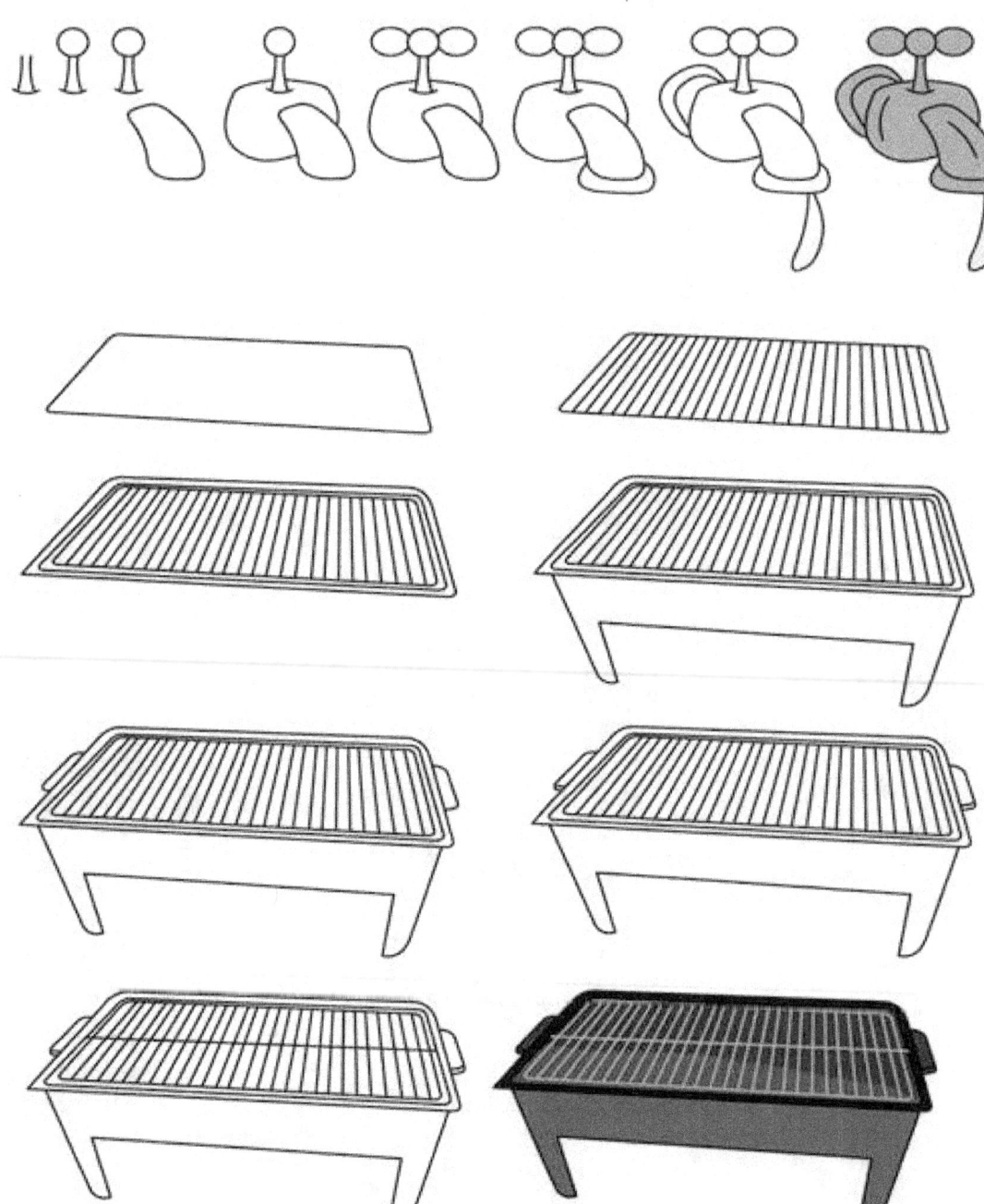

Let's redraw it on our own, my little artists

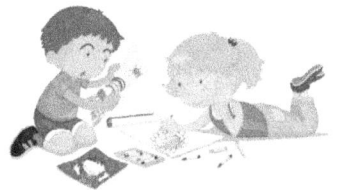

Let's Draw Our Garden

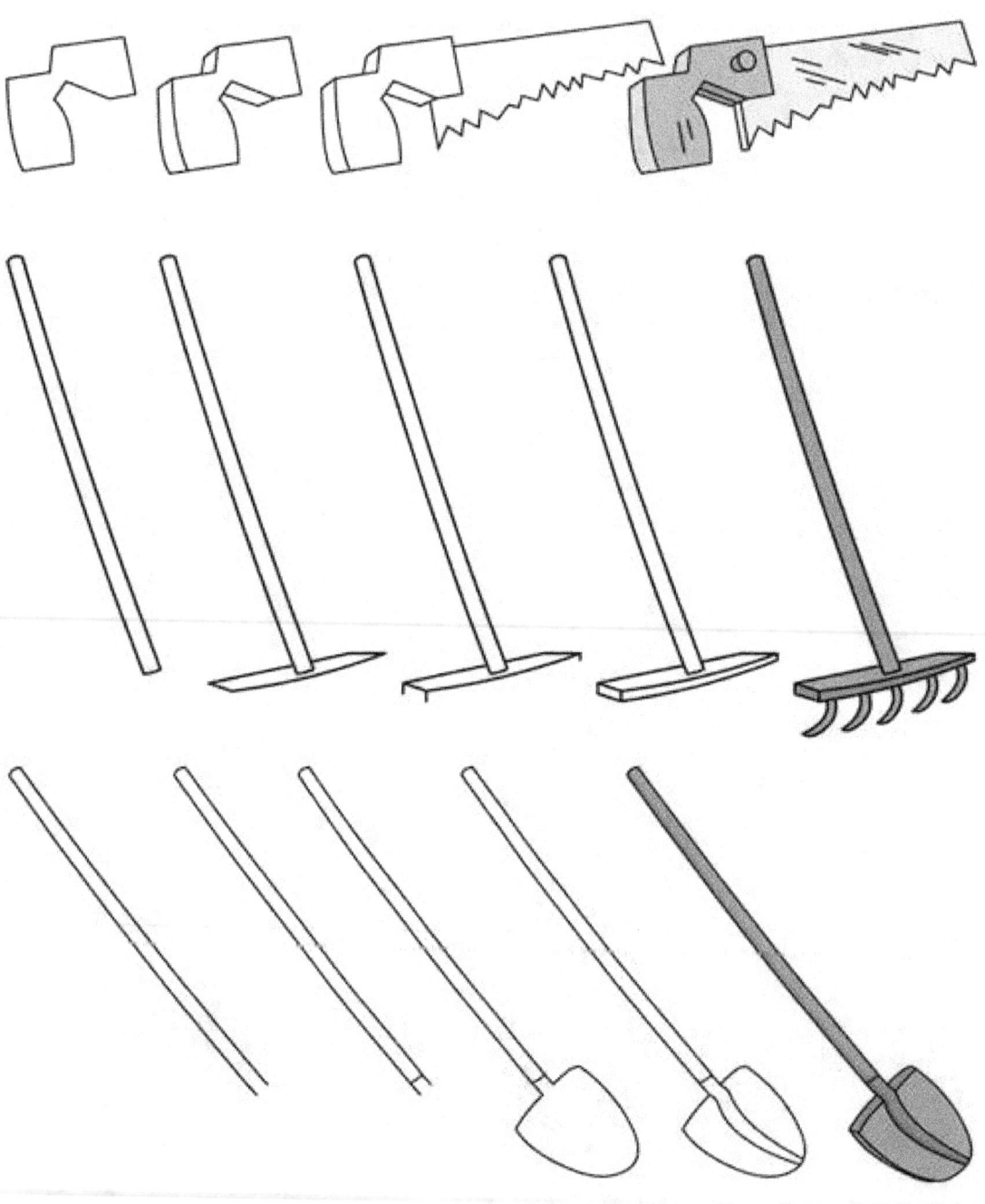

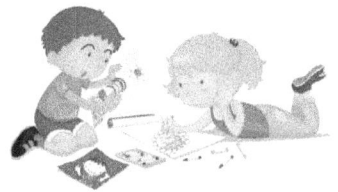

Let's redraw it on our own, my little artists

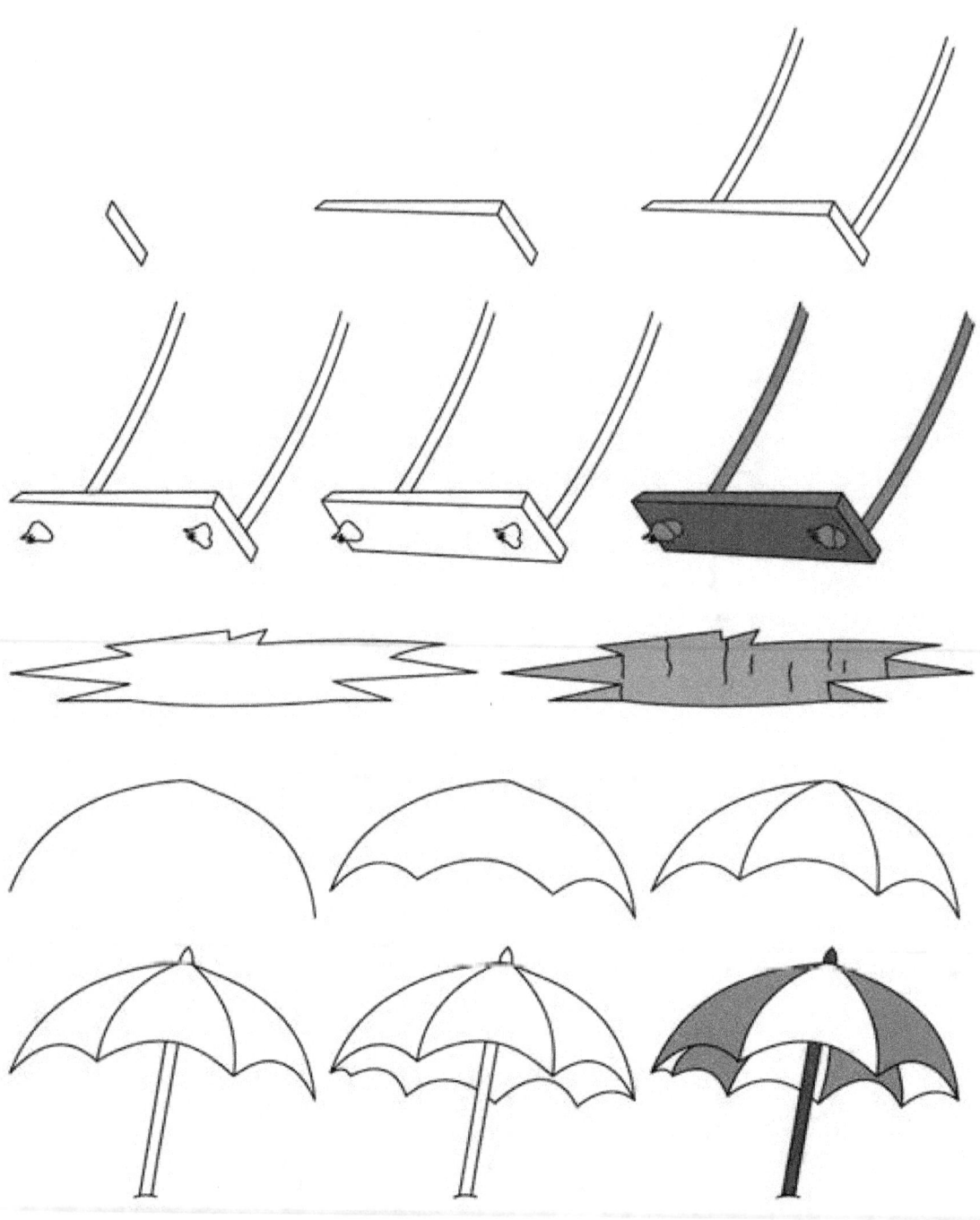

Let's redraw it on our own, my little artists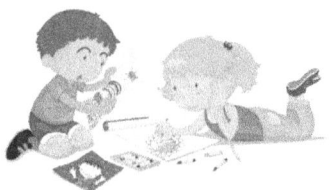

Let's Draw Our Garden

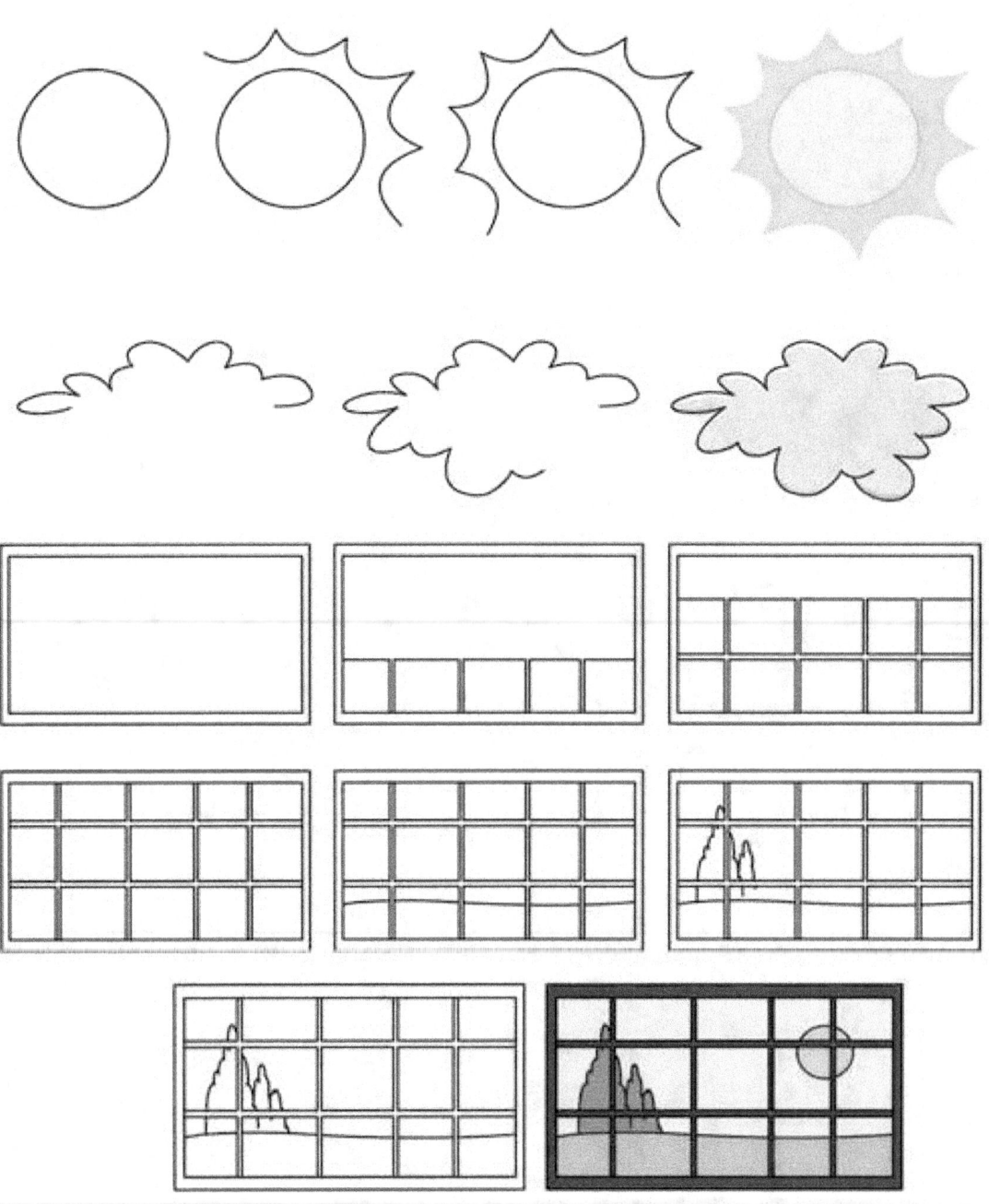

Let's redraw it on our own, my little artists

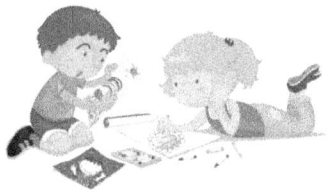

Let's Draw Our Garden

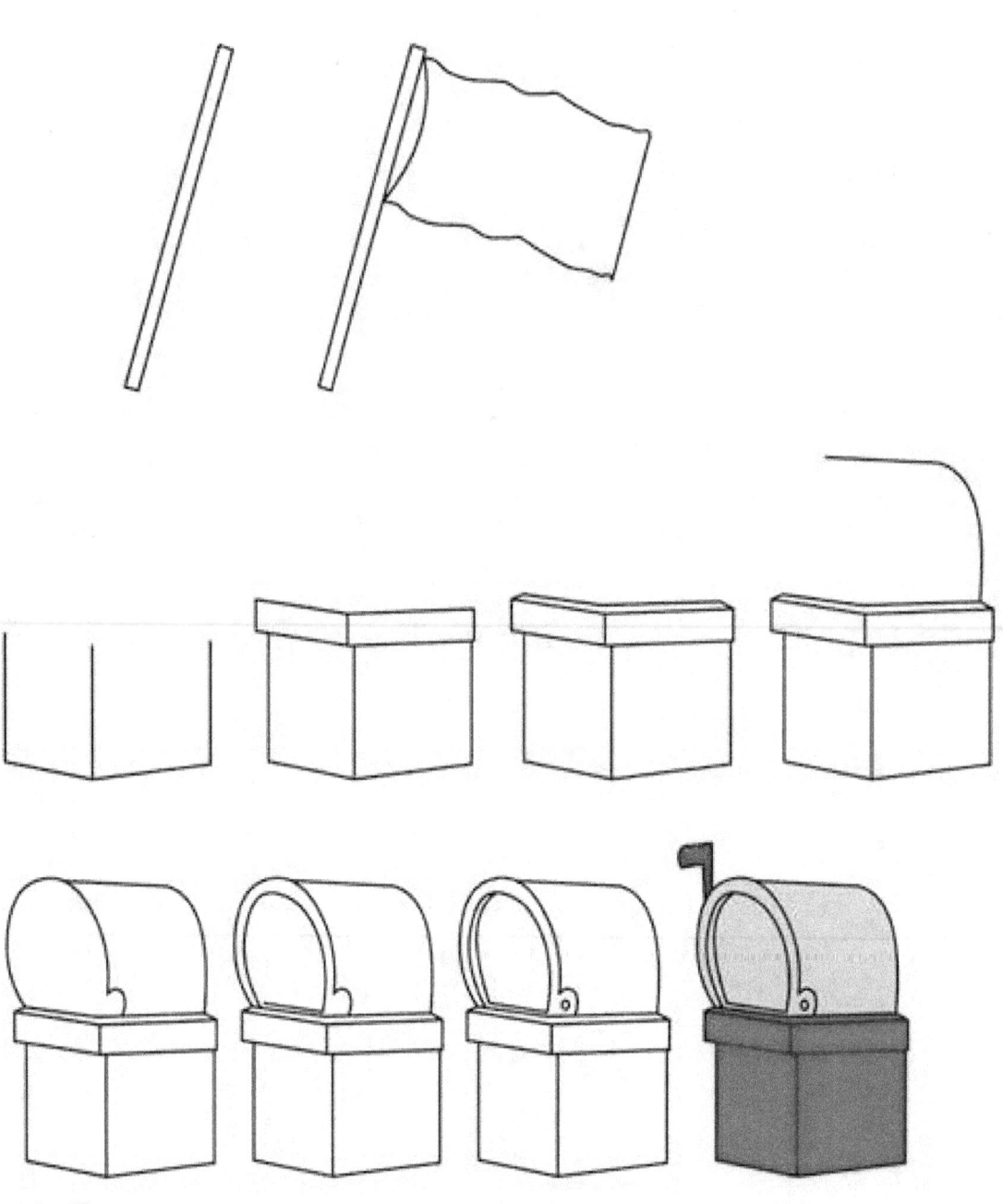

Let's redraw it on our own, my little artists

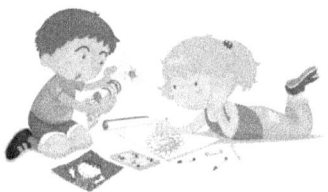

Let's Draw Our Garden

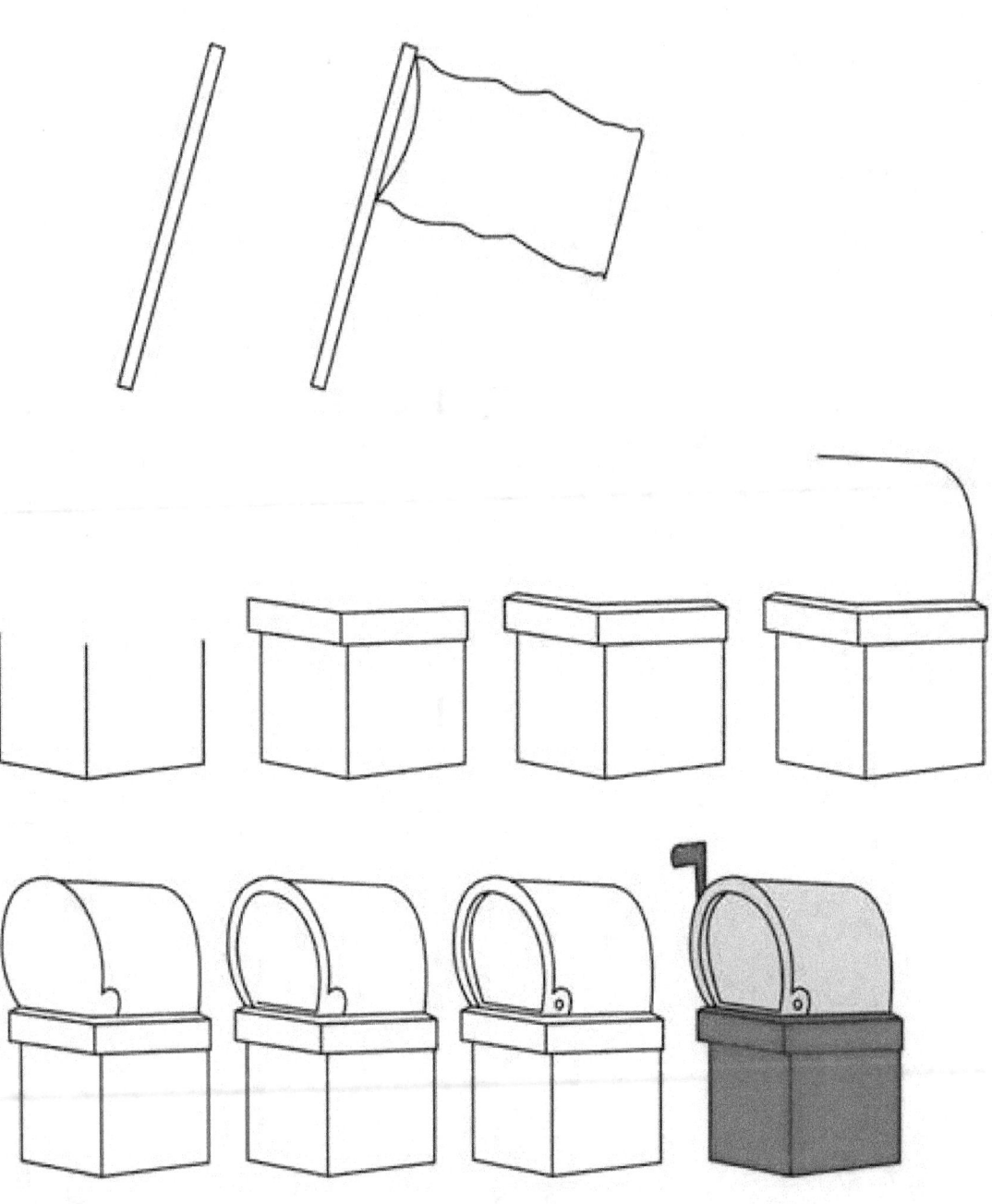

Let's redraw it on our own, my little artists

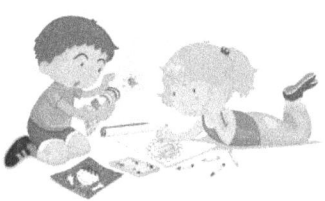